BEADWEAVING
BRILLIANCE

Many people are under the impression that beading stitches is both complicated and difficult, but it is neither. This beadweaving with needle and thread and its techniques have been handed down from generation to generation. Over the centuries, a number of stitches have been created, all of which have variations. But the basics are quite simple and can be mastered by anyone, which is why the craft is so popular all over the world.

We offer this book and its collection of jewelry that is easy and fun to make. Our designs use very basic stitches and techniques. You will find that the work goes quickly — none of the pieces takes longer than two hours to make. We have endeavored to provide clear, easy-to-follow instructions. Once you've mastered the basics and experienced the joys of this craft, you may find that you too have become an beading stitches addict!

Happy beading!

Kumiko Mizuno Ito
Author

C O N T E N T S

- -
Read the notes below before you
begin a project.
- -

· To make the jewelry in this book, we
used products manufactured by Toho Co.,
Ltd. The product numbers shown in our
instructions are Toho product numbers.
- -

· We suggest purchasing a few more beads
than the number indicated for a project,
just to be on the safe side.
- -

· Follow the instructions for each project
in order, referring to the accompanying
drawings.
- -

· In the drawings, FP stands for fire-polished
beads.
- -

· The finished measurements referred to
in this book are just benchmarks. Try the
jewelry on while you are working on it,
and make any necessary adjustments by
adding or subtracting beads.
- -

· The techniques introduced in this book
are in common use, but the same results
can be achieved using other techniques.
- -

USING THIS BOOK TO ADVANTAGE

■ We've arranged this book so that you can
begin with any project. You can select a
project according to three criteria: (1) type
of jewelry, (2) type of stitch, and (3) amount
of time required.

■ Refer to the following pages for detailed
instructions for each stitch.

· **Peyote stitch** ······ 10, 12, 24, 26
· **Spiral rope stitch** ····· 38
· **Netting** ······ 48
· **Daisy chain stitch** ····· 50
· **Right-angle weave stitch** ····· 52
· **Ladder stitch** ······ 54
· **Herringbone stitch** ······ 54

■ Please read the information on p. 75 about
working with needle and thread before you
begin a project.

■ Project-at-a-glance charts

Instructions: **p.15** ——— Location of instructions
Peyote stitch ——— Stitch used
70 minutes ——— Estimated time required

Notes
1. The number in the "Estimated time
required" box is just that — an estimate.
The amount of time it actually takes will
depend on your skill level.
2. No instructions are provided for jewelry
marked "For reference only."
We apologize for any inconvenience.

Part 1

RINGS

We urge all of you who are new to off-loom beadweaving to start out by making a ring. The rings in this book are worked in a very basic stitch: peyote stitch. Feel free to make changes to our designs by adding or subtracting the number of stitches or rows. Most of the designs are simple, but can be varied in infinite ways by using different beads or adding decorative touches. These rings can be completed within a short period of time: 60-90 minutes. We hope you'll be inspired to make all of them.

Instructions: p.14

Peyote stitch
70 minutes

Twill Ring

Design: Yokote Aiko

Fire-polished beads and seed beads are combined to make the pattern of this ring, which resembles the weave of twill fabric.
The ring has a presence that is strong and refreshing at the same time. Use larger beads if you want a ring with more volume (you'll finish it sooner, too).

Instructions: p.10

Peyote stitch
60 minutes

Peridot Fountain Ring

Design: Kosaka Ayako

Even with the basic peyote stitch, you can create a glamorous ring simply by combining different types of beads. Here we've used larger seed beads and fire-polished beads to make a beautiful ring that even beginners can make easily. At the back of the photo is the same ring worked in different colors.

Butterfly Ring

Design: Aiai Mari

This design features flower and leaf beads, which combine to form a miniature flower garden over which a butterfly hovers. The butterfly bead will sway slightly every time your hand moves, creating a beautiful effect.

Instructions: **p.15**
Peyote stitch
80 minutes

Instructions: **p.12**
Peyote stitch
80 minutes

Forest's Bounty Ring

Design: Nakata Mika

This ring in autumn colors displays Nature's bounty: beads that look just like the berries of the forest. The spring variation features the new buds of the season.

(For reference only)

Peyote stitch

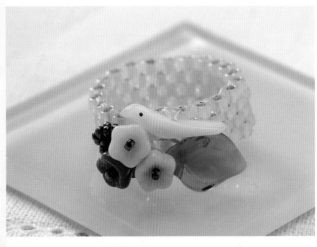

Flower-and-Bird Ring

Design: Sato Naomi

This ring features a lovely scene: a little bird perched on some flowers. The delicate band is worked in peyote stitch.

Bouquet Ring

Design: Okazoe Hiroko

The miniature bouquet will add a touch of elegance to your fingers. This is a voluminous ring, but we avoided even the slightest hint of heaviness by using beads in the same color family (flower beads, faceted beads and freshwater pearl beads).

(For reference only)

Peyote stitch

Instructions: **p.17**

Peyote stitch

80 minutes

Scattered Daisy Ring

Design: Koshimune Tamae

We used magatama beads interspersed with twisted hex beads to form the daisy centers. The petals surrounding the centers are seed beads. Why not try using different colors for the centers, or changing the number of petals?

Instructions: **p.16**

Peyote stitch

90 minutes

Flower Ring

Design: Umezawa Chiyo

To a simple band worked in peyote stitch we added seed-bead loops, arranging them so they look like flowers. Be creative with colors for the loops.

Instructions: **p.18**
Right-angle weave stitch
60 minutes

Cubic Zirconia Ring

Design: Akiyama Yoshie

The right-angle weave stitch involves working a series of figure eights. For the band of this stately ring, we chose color schemes that complement the cubic zirconia.

Peridot Fountain Ring

(Also shown on p. 5)

■Finished measurements:

1.3cm W x 6cm L

■Supplies

· 1.4m beading thread (see p. 74)
· 40 3-mm round fire-polished beads (olivine VA) #α-6603-96
· 40 3-mm seed beads (dark bronze) #83 (A)
· 40 3-mm seed beads (gold-lined translucent) #994 (B)

1 Make the band, working in peyote stitch.

❶String a stopper bead on thread, leaving a 20-cm end. Add beads in this order: one A bead (dark bronze seed bead), one B bead (transparent/light gold seed bead), 2 fire-polished beads, one B bead and one A bead (Fig. 1).

❷String one A bead, then pick up the B bead to the left of the right edge (Fig. 2).

❸Add a fire-polished bead and skip one fire-polished bead. String another fire-polished bead (Fig. 3).

❹String a B bead, skip the B bead from Step ①, and pick up the A bead at left edge. You have completed 6 rows of peyote stitch (Fig. 4).

❺Beginning with Row 4, add beads that are identical to the lowest beads in the previous row, passing the needle through the beads you skip (Fig. 5).

T I P S

①A stopper bead is a bead strung at the very beginning to keep the beads you add from falling off the thread. Remove it after you've finished weaving. (See p. 75 for instructions.)

②Our diagrams show the weaving process with the top of the woven piece facing you for clarity's sake. But feel free to work with the bottom facing you, if you prefer.

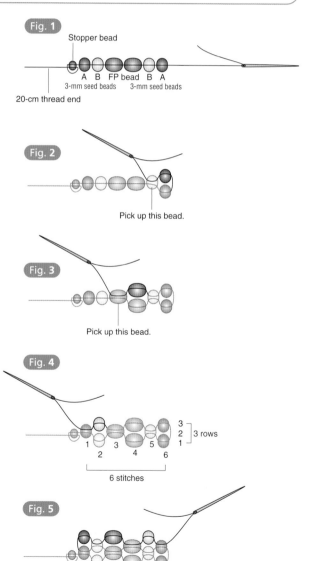

Fig. 1

Stopper bead

A B FP bead B A

3-mm seed beads   3-mm seed beads

20-cm thread end

Fig. 2

Pick up this bead.

Fig. 3

Pick up this bead.

Fig. 4

3
2   3 rows
1

1   3   5
2   4   6

6 stitches

Fig. 5

❻Repeat Step ⑤ until band is long enough to fit around your finger, ending at the edge without the stopper bead.

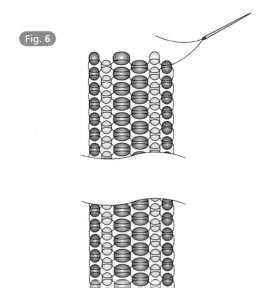

Fig. 6

TIP

Weave, in peyote stitch, the number of rows required to fit your finger, but be sure to end at the edge opposite the stopper bead.

---

② **Join edges of band and finish ring.**

❶Using the same thread, join edges of band by picking up beads protruding from each edge in alternation (Fig. 7).

❷Finish off thread: pick up first 3-mm seed bead strung, then pass needle through beads, forming intersections in two or three beads, as shown in drawing. Pull thread and cut excess at the edge of a bead (Fig. 8).

❸Finish off thread at starting point: remove stopper bead, run needle through beads as in Step ②, and cut excess thread (Fig. 9).

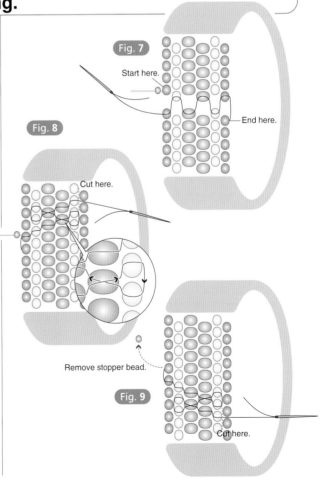

Fig. 7
Start here.
End here.

Fig. 8
Cut here.

Remove stopper bead.

Fig. 9
Cut here.

C o l o r   v a r i a t i o n
(Amethyst Fountain Ring)

■Supplies
· 40 3-mm round fire-polished beads (amethyst) #α-6603-7
· 40 3-mm seed beads (metallic purple) #85 (A)
· 40 3-mm seed beads (transparent/light gold) #994 (B)

Forest's Bounty Ring

(Also shown on p. 6)

■Finished measurements:

1.3cm W x 6cm L

■Supplies

· 2m beading thread (see p. 74)
· 259 2-mm seed beads (dark bronze) #222
· 4-mm round fire-polished bead (bronze) #α6604-41
· 5 x 6-mm glass pearl bead (orange) #α389-4
· 6-mm round glass pearl bead (reddish bronze) #α388-15
· 2 oval 5 x 9-mm handmade beads (topaz) #α5132-10
· 6-mm round handmade bead (red) #α5131-4
· 7-mm oval faceted-glass bead (orange)

① Make the band, working in peyote stitch.

❶String a stopper bead on thread, leaving a 20-cm end. Add 8 2-mm seed beads (Fig. 1).

❷String a seed bead, then pick up second seed bead to left of last bead strung in Step ① (Fig. 2).

❸String a seed bead. Skip one seed bead from Step ①, then pick up next seed bead (Fig. 3).

❹Repeat Step ③ twice. You now have three 8-stitch rows of peyote stitch (Fig. 4).

❺Add seed beads, one at a time, picking up the seed beads protruding from the previous row as you go along. Continue weaving until band is long enough to fit around your finger, ending at edge opposite stopper bead (Fig. 5).

❻Join edges of band by picking up beads protruding from each edge in alternation. Run needle diagonally through woven piece and bring out where shown in drawing. Use the same thread to make and attach the "berries" (Fig. 6).

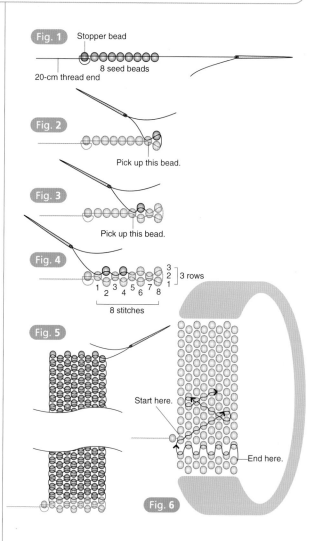

Fig. 1 Stopper bead
8 seed beads
20-cm thread end

Fig. 2 Pick up this bead.

Fig. 3 Pick up this bead.

Fig. 4 3 rows
1 2 3 4 5 6 7 8
8 stitches

Fig. 5 Start here.
End here.

Fig. 6

② Decorate the ring with berries.

❶String 2 seed beads, the bead indicated in drawing (first the reddish bronze glass pearl bead) and another seed bead. Pass needle back through all beads except seed bead last strung. Pick up seed beads at location shown in drawing. Make another berry with an oval handmade bead (Fig. 7).

❷Continue making berries in the same way, using the orange glass pearl bead, the fire-polished bead and the other oval handmade bead (Fig. 8).

❸Make two more berries, using the round handmade bead and then the oval faceted bead. String only one seed bead at the beginning of these (Fig. 9).

❹Pass needle through beads in band and finish off thread. Remove stopper bead and finish off thread at other end.

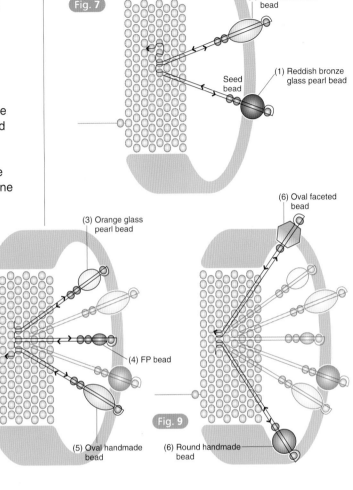

Fig. 7

(2) Oval handmade bead

(1) Reddish bronze glass pearl bead

Seed bead

(3) Orange glass pearl bead

Fig. 8

(4) FP bead

(5) Oval handmade bead

(6) Oval faceted bead

(6) Round handmade bead

Fig. 9

Color variations

Monochrome

■Supplies
- 259 2-mm seed beads (silver) #714
- 4-mm round fire-polished bead (silver crystal) #α6604-29
- 5 x 6-mm glass pearl bead (light gray) #α388-18
- 6-mm round glass pearl bead (black) #α389-16
- 2 5 x 9-mm oval handmade beads (transparent) #α5132-1
- Round 6-mm handmade bead (black) #α5131-18
- 7-mm oval faceted-glass bead (smoky quartz)

Green

■Supplies
- 259 2-mm seed beads (metallic yellow-green) #513
- 4-mm round fire-polished bead (olivine VA) #α6604-96
- 5 x 6-mm glass pearl bead (light orange) #α389-3
- 6-mm round glass pearl bead (light olive) #α388-13
- 2 5 x 9-mm oval handmade beads (dark green) #α5132-15
- 6-mm round handmade bead (green) #α5131-14
- 7-mm oval faceted-glass bead (olive)

Twill Ring

(Also shown on p. 5)

■Finished measurements:

1.3cm W x 6cm L

■Supplies

· 1.5m beading thread (see p. 74)
· 104 2-mm seed beads (red) #329
· 52 3-mm round fire-polished beads (red jasper) #α6603-55

❶String a stopper bead on thread, leaving a 20-cm end. Add fire-polished and seed beads as indicated in drawing (Fig. 1).

❷Add 2 seed beads and one fire-polished bead at a time, picking up fire-polished and seed beads in previous row, as shown in drawing (Figs. 2 and 3). Repeat Steps ② and ③ until band is desired length. End with 2 seed beads at edge opposite stopper bead.

❸Join edges of band, picking up beads protruding from each edge in alternation (Fig. 4).

❹Finish off thread at beginning and end of work.

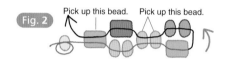

Fig. 1

FP bead

20-cm thread end   4 seed beads

Stopper bead

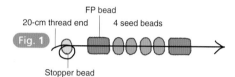
Fig. 2

Pick up this bead.   Pick up this bead.

Fig. 3

Fig. 4

Start here.

End here.

Color variations

Topaz

■Supplies

· 104 2-mm seed beads (bronze) #221
· 52 3-mm round fire-polished beads (mottled rose) #α6603-34

Purple

■Supplies

· 104 2-mm seed beads (black) #49
· 52 3-mm round fire-polished beads (mottled light amethyst) #α6603-35

Butterfly Ring

(Also shown on p. 6)

■Finished measurements:

0.8cm W x 6cm L

■Supplies

· 1.5m beading thread (see p. 74)
· 214 Aiko beads (blue) #781
· 2 Aiko beads (aurora) #161
· 7 x 9-mm butterfly bead (pale blue)
· 6 x 12-mm leaf bead (green)
· 10-mm flower bead (transparent)
· 10-mm flower bead (dark blue)
· 10-mm flower bead (pale blue)

*See p. 34 for supplies for pink and yellow rings.

❶String a stopper bead on thread, leaving a 20-cm end. String 8 blue Aiko beads (Fig. 1).

❷Add one Aiko bead at a time, picking up beads from the previous row as you go along (Figs. 2 and 3). Repeat this step until band is desired length, ending at edge opposite stopper bead.

❸Join edges of band, picking up beads protruding from each edge in alternation (Fig. 4).

❹Pick up first bead strung and run needle through band on the diagonal, referring to drawing. Bring needle out at center (Fig. 5).

❺String decorative beads A on thread extending from center, then pick up a Aiko bead on band. Attach B and C to band in the same way (Figs. 6 and 7).

❻Finish off threads at beginning and end of work.

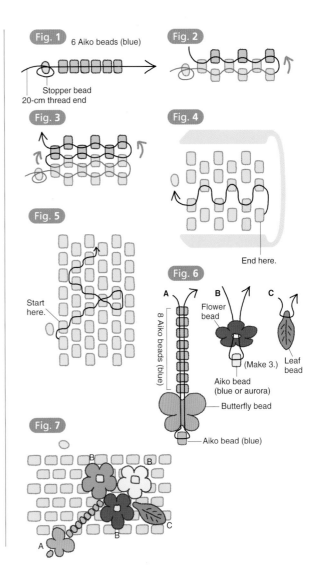

Flower Ring

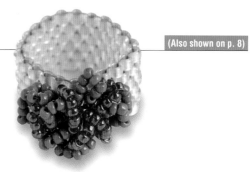

(Also shown on p. 8)

■Finished measurements:

1.3cm W x 6cm L

■Supplies

· 2m beading thread (see p. 74)
· 132 3-mm seed beads (matte white) #21F
· 80 2-mm seed beads (mauve) #52
· 50 2-mm seed beads (reddish purple) #332

*See p. 34 for supplies for blue ring.

❶String a stopper bead on thread, leaving a 20-cm end. String 6 3-mm seed beads (Fig. 1).

❷Add one 3-mm seed bead at a time, picking up beads from the previous row as you go along (Figs. 2 and 3). Repeat this step until band is desired length, ending at edge opposite stopper bead.

❸Join edges of band, picking up beads protruding from edges in alternation (Fig. 4).

❹Pick up first bead strung and run needle through band on the diagonal, referring to drawing. Bring needle out at center (Fig. 5).

❺String 8-10 mauve seed beads on thread extending from center. Pick up a 3-mm seed bead on band to form a loop (Fig. 6).

❻Repeating Step ⑤, make 5-6 loops with reddish purple seed beads and 8-10 more loops with mauve seed beads, and attach to band (Figs. 6 and 7).

❼Finish off threads at beginning and end of work.

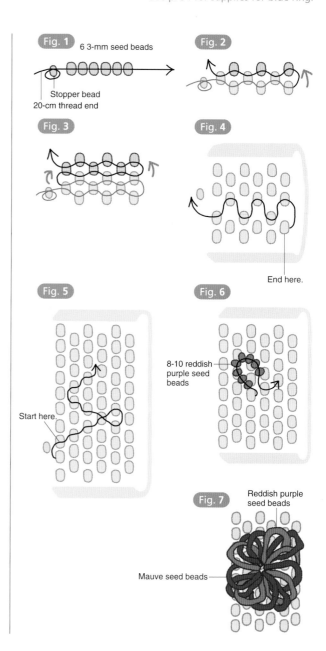

Fig. 1   6 3-mm seed beads

Stopper bead
20-cm thread end

Fig. 2

Fig. 3

Fig. 4

End here.

Fig. 5

Start here.

Fig. 6

8-10 reddish purple seed beads

Fig. 7   Reddish purple seed beads

Mauve seed beads

Scattered Daisy Ring

(Also shown on p. 8)

■Finished measurements:
1.3cm W x 6cm L

■Supplies
· 1.6m beading thread (see p. 74)
· 168 2-mm twisted hex beads (matte blue-green) #707
· 60 2-mm seed beads (white) #762
· 5 4-mm magatama beads (blue) #M28

*See p. 34 for supplies for purple ring.

❶String a stopper bead on thread, leaving a 20-cm end. String 6 twisted hex beads (Fig. 1).

❷Add one twisted hex bead at a time, picking up beads on previous row as you go along (Figs. 2 and 3).

❸Between Rows 10 and 25, add a magatama bead instead of a twisted hex bead where indicated in drawing. Magatama beads will form centers of daisies (Fig. 4). After Row 25, repeat Step ② until band is desired length, ending at edge opposite stopper bead.

❹Join edges of band, picking up beads protruding from each edge in alternation (Fig. 5).

❺Pick up first bead strung and run needle through band on the diagonal, referring to drawing. Bring needle out next to first magatama bead strung (Fig. 6).

❻String 12 seed beads on thread, then pass needle through first 6 seed beads strung to make the petals (Fig. 7).

❼Pass needle through magatama bead and twisted hex beads on band. Bring needle out and tack petals to band in two places. Pass needle through magatama bead again (Figs. 7 and 8).

❽Finish off threads at beginning and end of work.

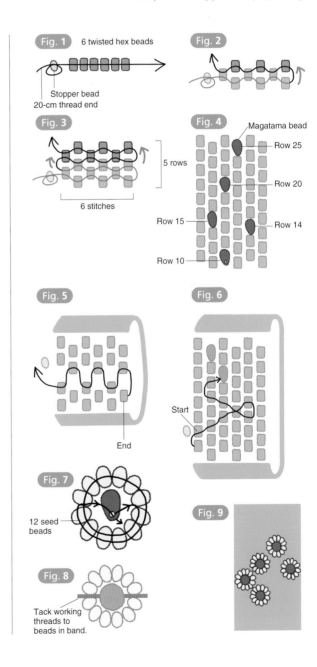

Fig. 1 — 6 twisted hex beads
Stopper bead
20-cm thread end

Fig. 2

Fig. 3 — 6 stitches

Fig. 4 — Magatama bead
Row 25
Row 20
5 rows
Row 15
Row 14
Row 10

Fig. 5

Fig. 6 — Start / End

Fig. 7 — 12 seed beads

Fig. 8 — Tack working threads to beads in band.

Fig. 9

Cubic Zirconia Ring

(Also shown on p. 9)

■Finished measurements:

0.8cm W x 6cm L

■Supplies

· 5.5m beading thread (see p. 74)
· 8-mm rectangular cubic zirconia (purple) #α6073-6
· 10 4-mm round fire-polished beads (mottled light amethyst) #α6603-35
· 4 6-mm bugle beads (purple) #85
· 4 3-mm cube beads (purple) #703
· 21 3-mm seed beads (purple) #88 (A)
· 8 3-mm seed beads (lavender) #328 (B)
· 28 2-mm seed beads (purple) #88 (a)
· 64 2-mm seed beads (lavender) #328 (b)

*See p. 34 for supplies for red and green rings.

❶String a stopper bead on thread, leaving a 20-cm end. String a 2-mm seed bead (a), a fire-polished bead, and the cubic zirconia. Pick up all the beads, starting with the 2-mm seed bead (a), and moving in the same direction. Pull thread (Figs. 1 and 2).

❷Add cube beads, 2-mm seed beads (b) and bugle beads as shown in drawing. Work around cubic zirconia, picking up beads already strung (Fig. 3).

❸String one 2-mm seed bead (b) at a time where indicated in drawing. Work around cubic zirconia, picking up beads already strung (Fig. 4).

❹Now add beads for Round 2 along outside edges. String 2-mm seed beads (a), 3-mm seed beads (B) and bugle beads where shown in drawing, picking up cube and fire-polished beads from Round 1 (Fig. 5).

❺Pass needle through beads in Rounds 1 and 2 to complete top of ring. Bring needle out through 3-mm seed bead indicated in drawing, and begin weaving band (Fig. 6).

❻Add a fire-polished bead, then pass needle through 3-mm seed bead (B), fire-polished bead and other 3-mm seed bead protruding from Round 2, and back through fire-polished bead just strung. Add 2 2-mm seed beads (a), a 3-mm seed bead (A), 2 more 2-mm seed beads (b) and a fire-polished bead. Pick up a fire-polished bead, 2 2-mm seed beads (b) and a 3-mm seed bead (A). Continue in same way, alternating between 3-mm seed beads and fire-polished beads, until band is desired length. Pick up fire-polished bead in Round 2 of top (Fig. 7).

❼Add one 2-mm seed bead (a) and one 3-mm seed bead (B) at a time to bottom of band. When you reach the cubic zirconia, pass needle through fire-polished bead indicated on drawing. Then add same beads to top of band (Fig. 8).

❽Run needle through beads in band and top of ring, making several half-hitch knots as you go. Remove stopper bead from beginning of work and finish off thread in the same way.

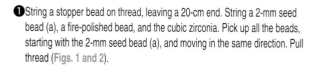

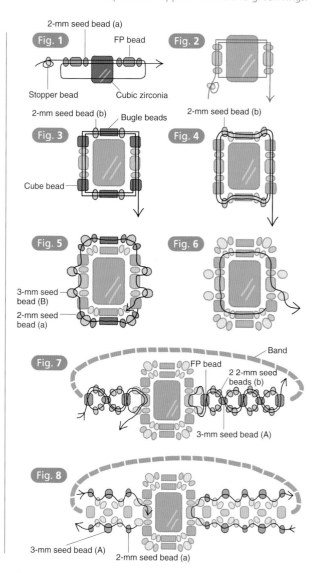

Fig. 1 — 2-mm seed bead (a), FP bead, Stopper bead, Cubic zirconia

Fig. 2

Fig. 3 — 2-mm seed bead (b), Bugle beads, Cube bead

Fig. 4 — 2-mm seed bead (b)

Fig. 5 — 3-mm seed bead (B), 2-mm seed bead (a)

Fig. 6

Fig. 7 — FP bead, 2 2-mm seed beads (b), Band, 3-mm seed bead (A)

Fig. 8 — 3-mm seed bead (A), 2-mm seed bead (a)

Part 2

PENDANTS

Necklaces and chokers are high on our list of jewelry to make. But pendants are an excellent first step in this direction. You can simply attach them to a purchased chain or leather cord, so they can be made in a relatively short time. Most of the pendants in this book are made using the peyote stitch, like the rings in the previous section. By working in tubular peyote stitch, or adding fringe, you can create a multitude of variations.

Lamina Pendant

Design: Matsumoto Makiko

To make this pendant, we wove two square lamina (plates) in beads of contrasting colors, and fastened them together. Bugle beads accentuate the beautiful peyote stitch pattern. They also make the stitch more accessible to beginners. Your pendant will be finished in no time!

Instructions: **p.24**

| Peyote stitch |
| 90 minutes |

Instructions: **p.28**

| Peyote stitch |
| 80 minutes |

Lampwork Bead Pendant

Design: Sato Kazue

This pendant features a diamond-shaped base topped with a pearl bead mounted on a lacy filigree flower. Two strands of fringe with lampwork beads at their ends are suspended from the base. The fringe will sway gently with your every move.

Instructions: **p.26**

| Peyote stitch |
| 80 minutes |

Fringed Pendant

Design: Yamaguchi Akiko

Made in peyote stitch like the band of a ring, this pendant has long strands of fringe cascading from it. You can make them even longer, if you like. You can also create any number of variations just by changing the colors of the beads.

Instructions: **p.29**

Peyote stitch

90 minutes

Temple Bell Pendant

Design: Ichimura Sachiko

Magatama beads are scattered among seed beads in the three peyote-stitch cylinders in this pendant, inspired by temple bells. You could, of course, make the pendant with just one cylinder. Make another and decorate your handbag with it.

Nested Pearl Pendant

Design: Watanabe Waka

Here we have a pearl bead partially hidden by a bead nest. Twisted hex beads join other beads to form a ladder-stitch cylinder (the nest). You could use chain for the necklace, but for a more harmonious piece, we suggest stringing some of the same beads used to make the pendant on wire.

Instructions: **p.30**

Ladder stitch

100 minutes

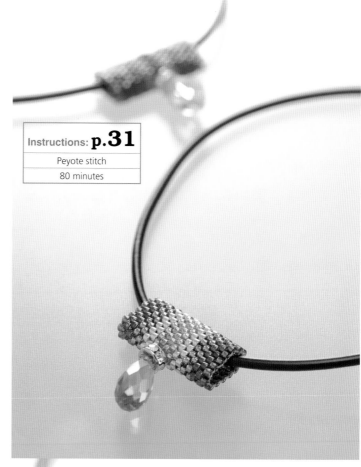

Instructions: **p.31**

| Peyote stitch |
| 80 minutes |

Striped Choker

Design: Yoshihara Kazuko

This is a simple design: just a peyote-stitch cylinder graced with a topaz drop bead. The subtle color changes make this choker even more spectacular. Surely you'll want to make a matching ring!

Instructions: **p.32**

| Peyote stitch |
| 90 minutes |

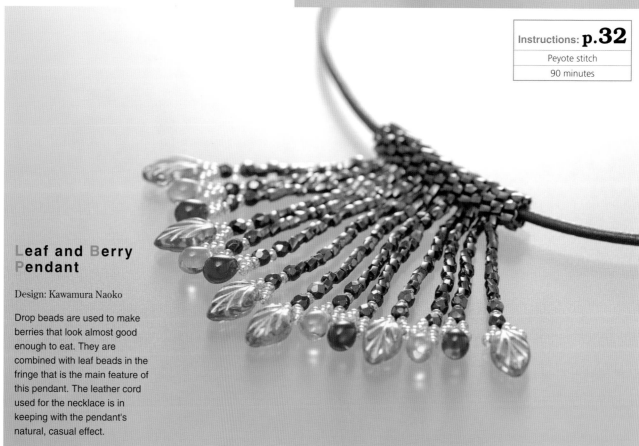

Leaf and Berry Pendant

Design: Kawamura Naoko

Drop beads are used to make berries that look almost good enough to eat. They are combined with leaf beads in the fringe that is the main feature of this pendant. The leather cord used for the necklace is in keeping with the pendant's natural, casual effect.

Choker with Leather Cord and Matching Earrings

Design: Hayashi Naoko

The pieces in this set begin with peyote-stitch cylinders. Larger beads are then added, creating a striking effect. This is a case where the beads, the materials they're made from, and the colors add up to much more than the sum of their parts.

Lamina Pendant

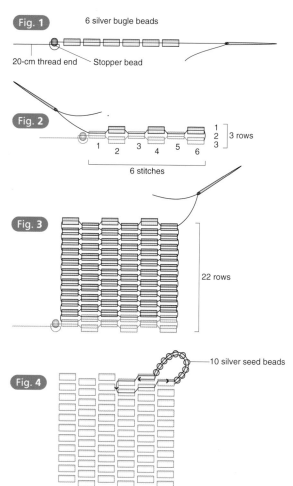

(Also shown on p. 19)

■Finished length (pendant):

4cm

■Supplies

· 2.8m beading thread (see p. 74)
· 66 3-mm bugle beads (silver) #Royal 713
· 128 3-mm bugle beads (matte bronze) #Royal 614
· 20 1.5-mm seed beads (silver) #714
· 13 1.5-mm seed beads (transparent) #1
· 6-mm bicone Swarovski crystal bead (crystal) #1
· 6 x 9-mm teardrop Swarovski crystal bead (crystal) #J-63-1
· Bail (silver) #9-13-7S
· 50cm 1.5-mm diamond-cut ball chain (silver) #α655-S

1 Weave two plates, using peyote stitch.

❶Make small plate: cut 1m thread. String a stopper bead on thread, leaving a 20-cm end. Add 6 silver bugle beads (**Fig. 1**).

❷String another silver bugle bead. Skip a bugle bead strung in Step ①, then add a new bead. Repeat. You now have 3 6-stitch rows (**Fig. 2**).

❸On Row 4, pick up the beads protruding from previous row, adding one bugle bead at a time. Weave until you have 22 rows (**Fig. 3**).

❹String 10 silver 1.5-mm seed beads on same thread. Pick up bugle beads where indicated in drawing to form a loop. Run needle through loop once more for added strength. Finish off threads at beginning and end of plate (**Fig. 4**).

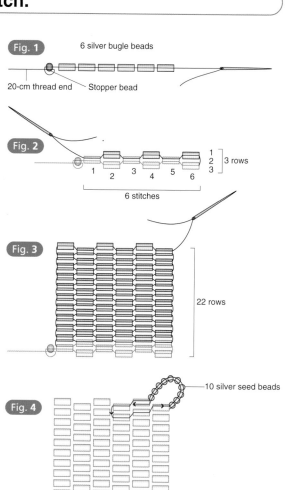

Fig. 1 — 6 silver bugle beads / 20-cm thread end / Stopper bead

Fig. 2 — 6 stitches / 3 rows

Fig. 3 — 22 rows

Fig. 4 — 10 silver seed beads

❺For larger plate, cut 1.3m thread and follow instructions in Steps ① - ④. Work in peyote stitch using bronze bugle beads on 8 stitches until you have 32 rows. Make a loop with 10 silver 1.5-mm seed beads (Fig. 5).

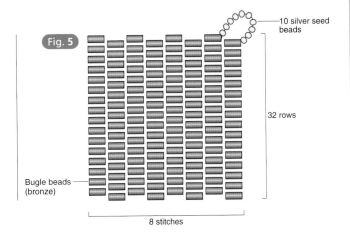

Fig. 5

10 silver seed beads

32 rows

Bugle beads (bronze)

8 stitches

2 Make ornament.

❶Cut 50cm thread. String 10 transparent 1.5-mm seed beads on thread, leaving a 15-cm end. Run needle through beads again in same direction to form a loop (Fig. 6).

❷String a bicone crystal bead, a teardrop crystal bead and 3 transparent 1.5-mm seed beads. Pass needle back through teardrop and bicone beads (Fig. 7).

❸Tie a square knot with threads at beginning and end. Hide thread ends in beads. Pull on thread until knot slips inside beads; cut excess thread at the edge of a bead (Fig. 8).

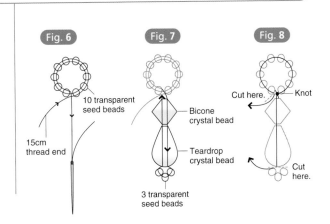

Fig. 6

10 transparent seed beads

15cm thread end

Fig. 7

Bicone crystal bead

Teardrop crystal bead

3 transparent seed beads

Fig. 8

Cut here. Knot

Cut here.

3 Attach chain.

❶Attach small and large plates and ornament to bail. Thread chain through bail. Turn small plate over so that beads are facing in the opposite direction of those on larger plate (Fig. 9).

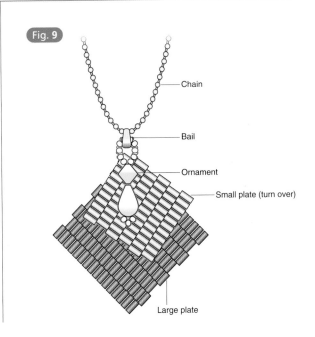

Fig. 9

Chain

Bail

Ornament

Small plate (turn over)

Large plate

Fringed Pendant

(Also shown on p. 20)

■Finished length (pendant):

1.5cm W x 3.5cm L

■Supplies

· 1.3m beading thread (see p. 74)
· 8 3-mm round fire-polished beads (azuro-coated ruby) #α6603-89
· 8 4-mm round fire-polished beads (azuro-coated ruby) #α6604-89
· 70 2-mm seed beads (iridescent dark brown) #83
· 84 2-mm seed beads (green) #991
· 54 2-mm seed beads (beige) #948
· 45cm cable chain necklace with clasp (gold) #12-1-2G

1 Make peyote-stitch rectangle.

❶String a stopper bead on thread, leaving a 20-cm end. String 10 green seed beads on thread to complete Rows 1 and 2 (**Fig. 1**).

❷Changing the color of the seed beads every two rows, weave in peyote stitch until you have 24 10-stitch rows (**Fig. 2**).

❸Picking up beads protruding from edges of woven piece, join edges, alternating between one edge and the other. Pick up seed beads and bring needle out where indicated in drawing (**Fig. 3**).

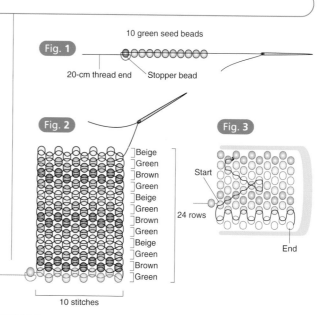

Fig. 1

10 green seed beads

20-cm thread end   Stopper bead

Fig. 2

Beige
Green
Brown
Green
Beige
Green
Brown
Green
Beige
Green
Brown
Green

10 stitches

Fig. 3

Start

24 rows

End

Color variations

Red

■Supplies

· 8 3-mm round fire-polished beads (fuchsia) #α6603-32
· 8 4-mm round fire-polished beads (fuchsia) #α6604-32
· 54 2-mm seed beads (iridescent purple) #85
· 84 2-mm seed beads (reddish purple) #331
· 70 2-mm seed beads (dark pink) #356
· 45cm cable chain necklace with clasp (silver) #12-1-2S

Brown

■Supplies

· 8 3-mm round fire-polished beads (mottled rose) #α6603-34
· 8 4-mm round fire-polished beads (mottled rose) #α6604-34
· 54 2-mm seed beads (bronze) #221
· 84 2-mm seed beads (brown) #941
· 70 2-mm seed beads (topaz) #2
· 45cm cable chain necklace with clasp (gold) #12-1-2G

② Attach fringe to woven rectangle.

❶String a seed bead and a fire-polished bead on thread extending from pendant, as shown in drawing. Pass needle back through beads (except for beige seed beads) and pick up a seed bead from pendant (Fig. 4).

❷Make three more strands of fringe, following directions in Step ①. Bring needle out from a seed bead at right edge of pendant (Fig. 5).

❸Pass needle through seed beads in bottom row of pendant and bring it out where shown in drawing. Make 4 more strands of fringe, following directions in Steps ① and ② (Fig. 6). Finish off thread ends at beginning and end of work.

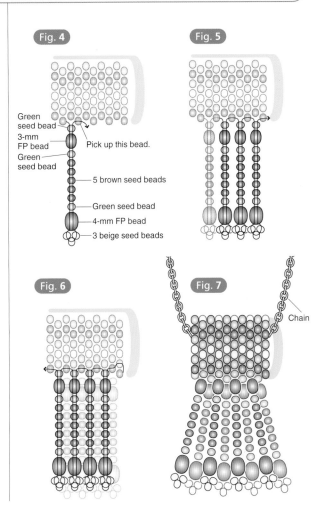

Fig. 4

Green seed bead
3-mm FP bead
Green seed bead
Pick up this bead.
5 brown seed beads
Green seed bead
4-mm FP bead
3 beige seed beads

Fig. 5

Fig. 6

Fig. 7

Chain

Color variations

Blue

■Supplies
· 8 3-mm round fire-polished beads (dark aqua) #α6603-12
· 8 4-mm round fire-polished beads (dark aqua) #α6604-12
· 54 2-mm seed beads (iridescent dark blue) #82
· 84 2-mm seed beads (azure) #87
· 70 2-mm seed beads (blue-violet) #168
· 45cm cable chain necklace with clasp (silver) #12-1-2S

White

■Supplies
· 8 3-mm round fire-polished beads (chalk white) #α6603-54
· 8 4-mm round fire-polished beads (chalk white) #α6604-54
· 54 2-mm seed beads (white) #981
· 84 2-mm seed beads (white) #2100
· 38 2-mm seed beads (aurora) #161*
· 32 2-mm seed beads (silver) #714*
· 45cm cable chain necklace with clasp (silver) #12-1-2S
*Mix these beads and use them where iridescent dark brown seed besds are called for in instructions on p.26 and this page.

Lampwork Bead Pendant

(Also shown on p. 20)

■Finished length (pendant):

3cm W x 5.5cm L

■Supplies

· 1.5m beading thread (see p. 74)
· 100 2-mm twisted hex beads (russet) #177
· 28 2-mm seed beads (light blue-green) #952
· 2 8 x 11-mm diamond-shaped lampwork beads (brown/gold) #α 1981
· 6-mm round glass pearl bead (ivory) #α 388-1
· Bar-and-ring toggle clasp (antique gold) #α 4227GF
· 40cm twist chain (antique gold) #α 665GF
· 17-mm filigree flower (antique gold) #α 4333GF
· 2 4.5-mm jump rings (antique gold) #α 4253GF

❶String a stopper bead on thread, leaving a 30-cm end. Add 10 twisted hex beads (**Fig. 1**).

❷Add one twisted hex bead at a time, picking up beads from previous row, as shown in drawings (**Figs. 2 and 3**). Repeat, working in peyote stitch until you complete 20 rows.

❸String 4 seed beads, loop on toggle clasp, and 4 more seed beads on same thread to form a loop. Pick up twisted hex beads indicated in drawing, and pass needle through beads in loop again (**Fig. 4**).

❹Pass needle through twisted hex beads, moving diagonally, as shown in drawing. Bring needle out at center of piece (**Fig. 5**).

❺Make ornament: string filigree flower, a pearl bead and a seed bead on same thread. Pass needle back through pearl bead and filigree flower. Pass needle through twisted hex beads in woven piece, and then through ornament components once again for added strength. Pass needle back through beads in woven piece and finish off thread (**Fig. 6**).

❻Remove stopper bead. Attach fringe, using thread at beginning of work. String 11 seed beads, a lampwork bead and one more seed bead. Pass needle back through beads again, as shown in drawing. Run needle through beads in woven piece, then make second strand of fringe. Pass needle back through beads in woven piece and finish off thread (**Fig. 7**).

❼Attach jump rings to loops on bar and ring of toggle clasp. Attach chain to jump rings (**Fig. 8**).

*See p. 34 for supplies for silver pendant.

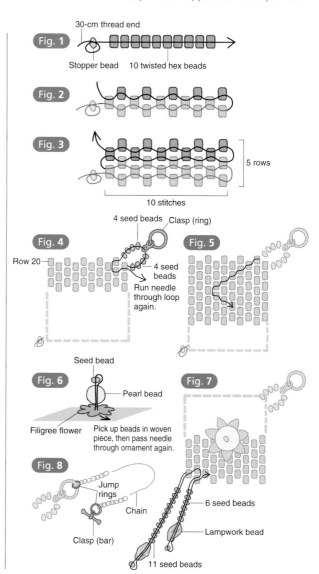

Temple Bell Pendant

(Also shown on p. 21)

■Finished length (pendant):
1cm W x 2.5cm L

■Supplies
- 1.5m beading thread (see p. 74)
- 62 3-mm seed beads (reddish purple) #332 (A)
- 31 3-mm seed beads (topaz) #103 (B)
- 21 2-mm seed beads (light red) #2113
- 26 4-mm magatama beads (light brown) #M02 (a)
- 13 4-mm magatama beads (brown) #M0202 (b)
- 45cm cable chain necklace (gold) #12-1-2-G

❶String a stopper bead on thread, leaving a 20-cm end. String 6 3-mm seed beads (A) on thread (**Fig. 1**).

❷Beginning with Row 3, add 3-mm seed beads (A) and magatama beads (a), referring to drawing. Weave in peyote stitch until you complete 12 rows (**Figs. 2, 3**).

❸Join edges of woven piece, picking up beads protruding from each edge in alternation. Pass needle back through beads (dotted lines in drawing), and bring it out where shown in drawing (**Fig. 4**).

❹String a magatama bead (a), 7 2-mm seed beads, and another magatama bead (a) on same thread to form a loop. Pass needle back through 3-mm beads in woven piece, as shown in drawing. Finish off thread (**Fig. 5**).

❺Remove stopper bead. String a magatama bead (a) on thread end at beginning of work. Pick up 3-mm seed beads in woven piece, as shown in drawing. String 5 more magatama beads in the same way, then pass needle back through beads in woven piece and finish off thread (**Fig. 6**).

❻Make the other two bells, referring to Steps ① - ⑤. Make one of them with 3-mm beads (B) and magatama beads (b).

❼Thread chain through the three bells (**Fig. 7**).

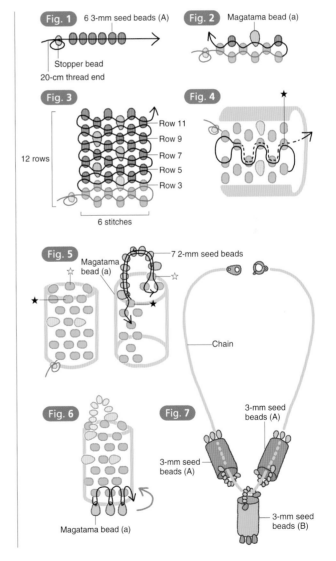

Fig. 1 — 6 3-mm seed beads (A)
Stopper bead
20-cm thread end

Fig. 2 — Magatama bead (a)

Fig. 3 — Row 11, Row 9, Row 7, Row 5, Row 3 — 12 rows — 6 stitches

Fig. 4

Fig. 5 — Magatama bead (a) — 7 2-mm seed beads — Chain

Fig. 6 — Magatama bead (a)

Fig. 7 — 3-mm seed beads (A) — 3-mm seed beads (A) — 3-mm seed beads (A) — 3-mm seed beads (B)

Nested Pearl Pendant

(Also shown on p. 21)

■ **Finished length (pendant):**

7.5cm

■ **Supplies**
- 2m beading thread (see p. 74)
- 10 12-mm twisted hex beads (matte blue-green) #707
- 59 3-mm seed beads (iridescent dark blue) #86 (includes 8 beads for necklace)
- 368 2-mm seed beads (light blue-green) #952 (includes 240 beads for necklace)
- 5-mm triangle bead (pale blue) #954
- 8-mm glass pearl bead (beige) #α499-14
- 5 5-mm glass pearl beads (beige) #α498-14 (includes 4 beads for necklace)
- 6 4 x 6-mm teardrop pressed-glass beads (pale green)
- 2 7 x 12-mm pressed-glass leaf beads (pale blue)

- Spring ring and chain tab set (gold) #9-1-1G
- 2 bead tips (gold) #9-4-1G
- 2 4.5-mm jump rings (gold) #α4253G
- 50cm beading wire with cord tips attached (gold) #α771

❶ String a twisted hex bead on thread, leaving a 30-cm end. Work 10 stitches in ladder stitch (follow Steps 1 ① - ③ on p. 54) (**Fig. 1**).

❷ Using the same thread, pick up first twisted hex bead strung at beginning of work, forming a cylinder (**Fig. 2**). Pass needle back through same beads for added strength. Bring thread end from beginning of work out from hole at opposite end of cylinder to use for fringe.

❸ String 4 2-mm seed beads, a 3-mm seed bead and 4 more 2-mm seed beads. Add beads for A fringe, as shown in drawing. Pass needle back through beads to pearl bead. Add 2-mm and 3-mm seed beads, then picking up beads indicated in drawing, make B, C and D fringe. Bring needle out at pearl bead (**Fig. 3**).

❹ String 2 3-mm seed beads, the 8-mm pearl bead and 9 3-mm seed beads. The 8-mm pearl bead should slip into the "nest," and 5 of the 3-mm seed beads should go inside the cylinder (**Fig. 4**).

❺ Add a 3-mm seed bead, the triangle bead and 11 3-mm seed beads. Pass needle back through same beads to make a loop. Add 3 3-mm seed beads; pick up twisted hex beads indicated in drawing and beads in loop while adding 3 3-mm seed beads six times. You should now have 2 twisted hex beads remaining (**Fig. 5**). Hide threads at beginning and end of work in twisted hex beads and finish off.

❻ Make necklace: string 2-mm seed beads, 3-mm seed beads and 5-mm pearl bead on beading wire, as shown in drawing. Attach a bead tip and a crimp bead to each end. Compress crimp beads (**Fig. 6**).

❼ Attach spring ring and chain tab to bead tips (**Fig. 7**).

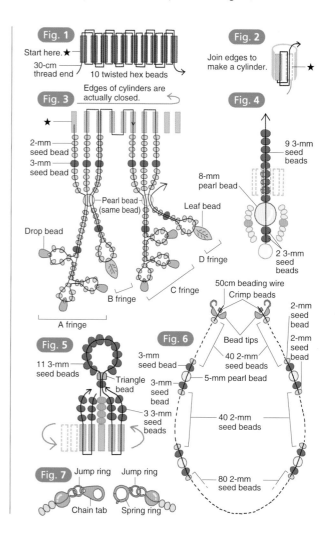

Striped Choker

(Also shown on p. 22)

■Finished measurements (woven piece):

2.5cm W x 4cm L

■Supplies
· 1.5m beading thread (see p. 74)
· 28 Aiko beads (topaz) #TB-103
· 28 Aiko beads (gold-lined translucent yellow) TB-22
· 56 Aiko beads (light gold) #TB-559
· 56 Aiko beads (gold-lined green) #TB-27
· 56 Aiko beads (deep green) #TB-796
· 28 Aiko beads (gold-lined blue-green) #TB-27BD
· 7 x 15-mm synthetic quartz drop bead (topaz)
· 5-mm rhinestone rondelle (crystal) #α630S
· Leather cord with lobster clasp, cord tips and jump rings (black/silver) #9-92B

*See p. 34 for supplies for blue choker.

❶String a stopper bead on thread, leaving a 20-cm end. String 18 Aiko beads (see **Fig. 1** for color arrangement).

❷Add one Aiko bead of the same color per stitch, while picking up beads from previous row (**Figs. 2 and 3**). Repeat until you have 28 rows of peyote stitch.

❸Join edges of woven piece as shown in drawings, picking up beads protruding from each edge in alternation. Pass needle back through beads diagonally, referring to drawing. Bring needle out at center (**Fig. 4**).

❹Make ornament: string rhinestone rondelle and quartz drop bead on same thread. Pass needle back through the two beads and through a few beads in woven piece. Pass needle through beads in ornament and back through beads in woven piece once again. Finish off thread (**Fig. 5**).

❺Remove stopper bead. Finish off thread at beginning of work (**Fig. 6**).

❻Thread leather cord through woven piece. Attach a cord tip to each end. Close cord tips with flat-nose pliers (**Fig. 6**).

❼Attach clasp and chain tab to cord tips with jump rings (**Fig. 7**).

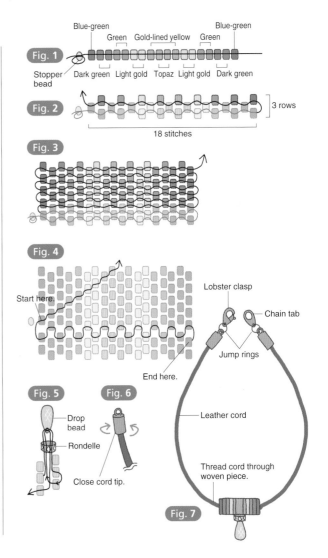

Leaf and Berry Pendant

(Also shown on p. 22)

■Finished measurements (pendant):

3.5cm W x 6.5cm L

■Supplies

· 2.3m beading thread (see p. 74)
· 316 2-mm twisted hex beads (metallic blue-green) #506
· 28 3-mm round fire-polished beads (antique brass) #α6603-42
· 98 2-mm seed beads (topaz) #103
· 4 4 x 6-mm pressed-glass drop beads (red)
· 4 4 x 6-mm pressed-glass drop beads (topaz)
· 6 7 x 12-mm pressed-glass leaf beads (yellow-green)
· Leather cord with lobster clasp, cord tips and jump rings (brown/antique bronze) #α8521

❶String a stopper bead on thread, leaving a 20-cm end. Add 16 twisted hex beads (**Fig. 1**).

❷Add one twisted hex bead at a time, picking up beads from previous row, as shown in drawings (**Figs. 2 and 3**). Repeat, working peyote stitch until you have 20 rows.

❸Join edges of woven piece by passing needle through protruding beads, one at a time, alternating between the two edges. Pass needle through first bead strung (**Fig. 4**).

❹Make 14 strands fringe: using same thread, string 12 twisted hex beads and Pattern A beads (a fire-polished bead, a seed bead, another fire-polished bead, 3 seed beads, a leaf bead and 3 more seed beads). Pass needle back through same beads and pick up a twisted hex bead from woven piece (**Fig. 5**).

❺For second strand of fringe, string 14 twisted hex beads and Pattern B beads (a fire-polished bead, a seed bead, another fire-polished bead, 3 more seed beads, a red drop bead and 3 more seed beads). For third strand, string 16 twisted hex beads and Pattern C beads (a fire-polished bead, a seed bead, another fire-polished bead, 3 more seed beads, a topaz drop bead and 3 more seed beads). Pass needle back through beads in fringe, as shown in drawing and pick up a twisted hex bead in woven piece (**Fig. 6**).

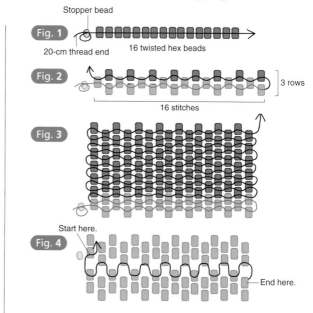

Stopper bead

Fig. 1

20-cm thread end   16 twisted hex beads

Fig. 2   3 rows

16 stitches

Fig. 3

Start here.

Fig. 4

End here.

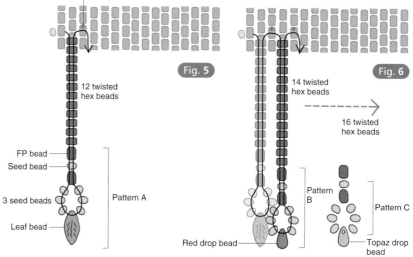

Pick up bead indicated by red dot.

12 twisted hex beads

FP bead
Seed bead

3 seed beads

Leaf bead

Pattern A

Fig. 5

14 twisted hex beads

Red drop bead

Pattern B

Fig. 6

16 twisted hex beads

Pattern C

Topaz drop bead

❻ake 7 strands of fringe, changing patterns and the number of twisted hex beads as directed. When you've finished the 7th strand, pick up twisted hex beads in woven piece and bring needle out where indicated in drawing. Make 7 more strands of fringe, changing patterns and the number of twisted hex beads as directed (**Fig. 7**). When you've finished the 14th strand, pick up twisted hex beads in woven piece and finish off thread.

❼Remove stopper bead. Finish off thread end at beginning of work.

❽Thread leather cord through woven piece. Attach a cord tip to each end. Close cord tips with flat-nose pliers (**Fig. 8**).

❾Attach clasp to one end and chain tab to other with jump rings (**Fig. 9**).

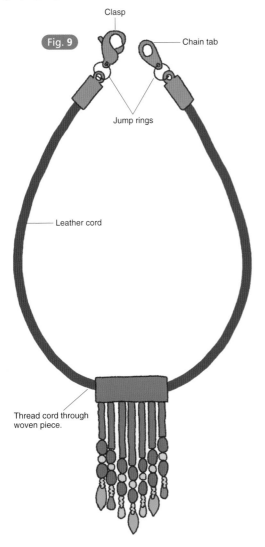

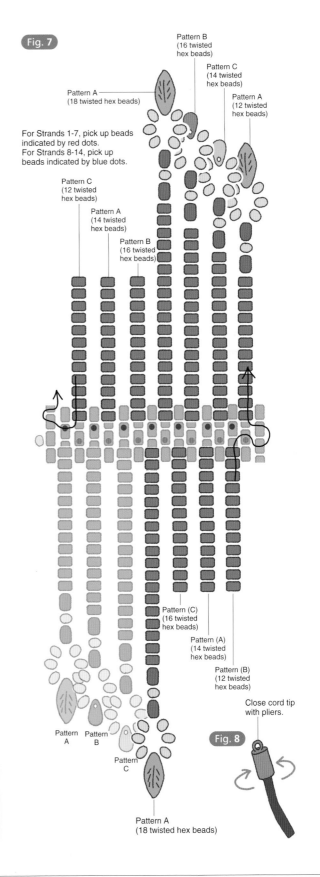

Supplies for color variations

(Please refer to main instructions for thread amounts.)

Butterfly Ring (pink)

`Instructions  p. 15`

· 214 Aiko beads (pink) #780
· 2 Aiko beads (aurora) #161
· 7 x 9-mm butterfly bead (transparent)
· 6 x 12-mm leaf bead (yellow-green)
· 2 10-mm flower beads (pink)
· 10-mm flower bead (transparent)

Butterfly Ring (yellow)

`Instructions  p. 15`

· 214 Aiko beads (aurora) #161
· 2 Aiko beads (blue) #781
· 7 x 9-mm butterfly bead (yellow)
· 6 x 12-mm leaf bead (yellow-green)
· 10-mm flower bead (transparent)
· 10-mm flower bead (orange)
· 10-mm flower bead (pale yellow)

Flower Ring

`Instructions  p. 16`

· 132 3-mm seed beads
  (matte black) #Ancient 2007
· 40 2-mm seed beads (turquoise) #55
· 100 2-mm seed beads (dark blue-green) #932

Daisy Ring

`Instructions  p. 17`

· 168 2-mm twisted hex beads
  (iridescent purple) #502
· 60 2-mm seed beads (white) #762
· 5 4-mm magatama beads (brown) #M46

Cubic Zirconia Ring (red)

`Instructions  p. 18`

· 8-mm rectangular cubic zirconia (red) #α6073-4
· 10 4-mm round fire-polished beads
  (antique brass) #α6604-42
· 4 6-mm bugle beads (purple) #82
· 4 3-mm cube beads (bronze) #221
· 29 3-mm seed beads (bronze) #221 ((A) and (B))
· 28 2-mm seed beads (bronze) #222 (a)
· 64 2-mm seed beads (aurora) #262 (b)

Cubic Zirconia Ring (green)

`Instructions  p. 18`

· 8-mm rectangular cubic zirconia
  (olive) #α6073-7
· 10 4-mm round fire-polished beads
  (olivine VA) #α6604-96
· 4 6-mm bugle beads (dark green) #84
· 4 3-mm cube beads (green) #710
· 21 3-mm seed beads (green) #322 (A)
· 8 3-mm seed beads (olive) #324 (B)
· 28 2-mm seed beads (green) #322 (a)
· 64 2-mm seed beads (olive) #324 (b)

Lampwork Bead Pendant (silver)

`Instructions  p. 28`

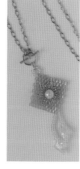

· 100 2-mm twisted hex beads
  (yellow-green aurora) #164
· 28 2-mm seed beads (cream) #948
· 2 8 x 11-mm diamond-shaped lampwork beads
  (silver) #α1978
· 6-mm round glass pearl bead (ivory) #α388-1
· Bar-and-ring toggle clasp (silver) #α4227S
· 40cm twist chain (silver) #α665S
· 17-mm filigree flower (silver) #α4333S
· 2 4.5-mm jump rings (silver) #α4253S

Striped choker (blue)

`Instructions  p. 31`

· 28 Aiko beads
  (matte red/blue/violet]) #TB-704
· 56 Aiko beads (blue-green) #TB-932
· 56 Aiko beads (translucent blue-green) #TB-7BD
· 56 Aiko beads (blue aurora) #TB-408
· 28 Aiko beads (translucent deep green) #TB-939
· 28 Aiko beads (translucent yellow-green) #TB-7
· 1.5-mm seed bead (crystal) #1
· 8 x 12-mm Swarovski crystal drop bead (crystal)
· 5-mm rhinestone rondelle (crystal) #α630S
· Leather cord with lobster clasp, cord tips and jump ring
  (black/silver) #9-92B

Part 3

STRAPS

Straps are items that we treasure, no matter how many we have. They make wonderful presents for friends or family members. Although they're often attached to cell phones, we're sure you'll think of many other uses for them. All the straps presented in this book are woven with the spiral rope stitch. One of the wonderful aspects of this stitch is that you can transform a design completely by using different beads. Once you've mastered the basic technique, you'll be ready to create original pieces.

Instructions: p.38

Spiral rope stitch

40 minutes

Bugle Bead Strap

Design: Segawa Tamami

This is a simple but fascinating design, with bugle-bead and fringe accents. This strap is also easy to make, so if you've never made one before, why not give it a try?

Seashore Strap

Design: Shiratori Madoka

This strap was inspired by the beautiful, pale blue color of the sea in early summer. It is made in almost the same way as the Garnet Spiral Strap below. Here, the core beads are 3-mm white seed beads, and the outer beads are blue fire-polished beads, 3-mm and gold-lined 1.5-mm seed beads.

Instructions: **p.40**

Spiral rope stitch

60 minutes

Garnet Spiral Strap

Design: Shiratori Madoka

The color scheme of this strap is almost diametrically opposite from that of the one shown above. Core beads are amethyst fire-polished beads, while bronze seed beads among the outer beads provide bold accents.

Instructions: p.40

Spiral rope stitch

60 minutes

Lavender Strap

Design: Kadota Yukiko

Lavender was the inspiration for this breathtakingly enchanting design, a combination of flowers and leaves. Blue and purple beads form the flowers, while the leaves are made with beads in various shades of green.

(For reference only)

Spiral rope stitch

Whirligig Strap

Design: Shimizu Miwako

This strap, also made with the spiral rope stitch, changes character easily. Make it in Christmas colors to brighten up your holidays, or in white for an elegant touch, or in purple for a royal look.

Bugle Bead Strap

(Also shown on p. 35)

■Finished length:

7.5cm (spiral: 6cm)

■Supplies

· 1.1m beading thread (see p. 74)
· 29 3-mm seed beads (dark reddish-purple) #331
· 71 2-mm seed beads (silver-lined translucent) #21
· 22 6-mm bugle beads (red) #332
· Strap finding with dual ring (black leather/silver) #6-3-30

1 Make the spiral rope.

❶String a stopper bead on thread, leaving a 40-cm end. Add 4 3-mm seed beads (core beads) (Fig. 1).

❷String outer beads (a 2-mm seed bead, a bugle bead and another 2-mm seed bead) (Fig. 2).

❸Pass needle through core beads again, starting with first bead strung. Pull thread so that outer beads are parallel to core beads (Fig. 3).

❹Add another core bead. Swing outer beads toward you to the left side of the core beads (Fig. 4).

❺String 3 outer beads. Pass needle through 4 top core beads from bottom, as you did in Step ③ (Fig. 5).

❻Repeat Steps ④ and ⑤ until you have a total of 22 spirals (Fig. 6).

TIP

As you repeat the spiral rope stitch, the outer beads wrap around the core beads to form spirals. It doesn't matter whether you turn the outer beads to the left or the right, but you should always move them in the same direction. You can control the way the beads wrap by adjusting thread tension when you pick up the core beads.

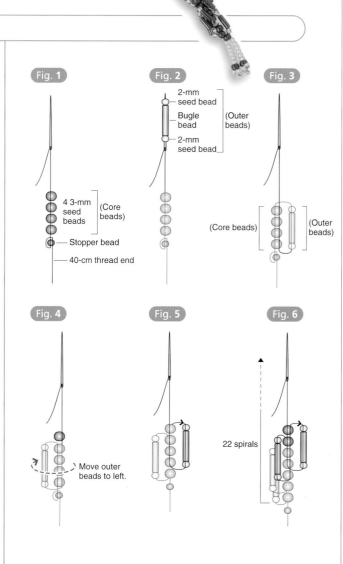

Fig. 1

4 3-mm seed beads (Core beads)
Stopper bead
40-cm thread end

Fig. 2

2-mm seed bead
Bugle bead (Outer beads)
2-mm seed bead

Fig. 3

(Core beads) (Outer beads)

Fig. 4

Move outer beads to left.

Fig. 5

Fig. 6

22 spirals

2 Attach strap finding.

❶ Add one 3-mm seed bead and 9 2-mm seed beads, using same thread. Pass needle through dual ring on strap finding. Pick up 3-mm seed bead, core bead and outer beads, referring to drawings. Pass needle through beads in loop through dual ring again (Fig. 7).

❷ Pick up core and outer beads, making several half-hitch knots as you go along. Finish off thread (Fig. 8).

T I P

When you're finishing off thread, make 2-3 half-hitch knots before and after passing needle through outer beads. Cut excess thread at the edge of a bead. (Directions for making a half-hitch knot are on p. 81.)

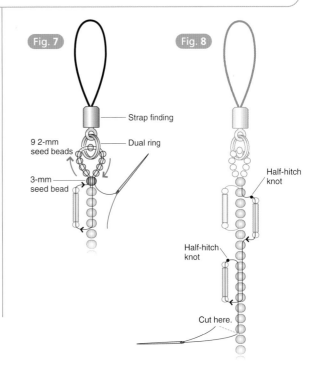

Fig. 7   Fig. 8

Strap finding

9 2-mm seed beads   Dual ring

3-mm seed bead

Half-hitch knot

Half-hitch knot

Cut here.

3 Attach fringe to bottom of strap.

❶ Remove stopper bead. Add a 3-mm seed bead, 6 2-mm seed beads, another 3-mm seed bead and 3 more 2-mm seed beads to thread end at beginning of work. Pass needle back through 3-mm seed bead and remaining beads on fringe (Fig. 9).

❷ Pass needle through core and outer beads indicated in drawing. Make second strand of fringe, following directions in Step ① (Fig. 10).

❸ Finish off thread, following directions in 2 ②.

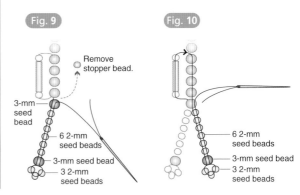

Fig. 9   Fig. 10

Remove stopper bead.

3-mm seed bead

6 2-mm seed beads

3-mm seed bead

3 2-mm seed beads

6 2-mm seed beads

3-mm seed bead

3 2-mm seed beads

Color variation

Blue ■Supplies
· 29 3-mm seed beads (dark blue) #2203
· 71 2-mm seed beads (silver-lined) #21
· 22 6-mm bugle beads (blue) #87
· Strap finding with dual ring (black leather/silver) #6-3-30

Garnet Spiral Strap

(Also shown on p. 36)

■Finished length: 17cm (spiral)

■Supplies
· 2m beading thread (see p. 74)
· 57 3-mm round fire-polished beads (amethyst) #α6603-7
· 52 3-mm round fire-polished beads (dark ruby) #α6603-8
· 104 3-mm seed beads (bronze) #221
· 326 1.5-mm seed beads (reddish purple) #332
· Strap finding with dual ring (black leather/silver) #6-3-30

❶String a stopper bead on thread, leaving a 20-cm end. String 4 amethyst fire-polished beads (core beads) on thread. Then string outer beads (1.5-mm seed beads, 3-mm seed beads, dark ruby fire-polished bead) (Fig. 1).

❷String another core bead, and move outer beads to left of core beads (Fig. 2).

❸String another set of outer beads, as in Step ①. Pass needle through top 4 core beads, starting at the bottom (Fig. 3). Repeat until you have 52 sets of outer beads.

❹String another core bead and 7 1.5-mm seed beads. Pass needle through dual ring on strap finding. Run needle back through beads again, forming a loop, as shown in drawing. Finish off thread, making half-hitch knots as you go along (Fig. 4).

❺Remove stopper bead. Add a core bead and 7 1.5-mm seed beads. Attach to dual ring on strap finding. Finish off thread.

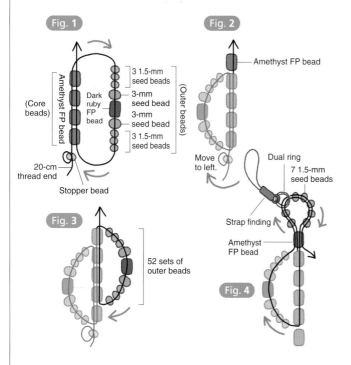

Lavender Strap

(Also shown on p. 37)

■Finished length: 16cm (spiral)

■Supplies
· 2m beading thread (see p. 74)
· 50 3-mm round fire-polished beads (soda blue) #α6603-42
· 25 4-mm round fire-polished beads (violet AB) #α6604-78
· 35 3-mm seed beads (blue-green) #264
· 25 3-mm seed beads (pink) #771
· 25 3-mm seed beads (blue) #774
· 35 2.2-mm triangle beads (deep green) #243
· 16 2-mm seed beads (green) #243
· 25 3-mm pearl beads (purple) #α-91
· 5 7 x 12-mm pressed-glass leaf beads (olive luster)
· Strap finding with dual ring (blue leather/silver) #6-3-28

❶String a stopper bead on thread, leaving a 20-cm end. Add 3 3-mm fire-polished beads (core beads). Then string A outer beads (triangle and 3-mm seed beads) (Fig. 1). Add another core bead and move outer beads to left (Fig. 2).

❷String another core bead, and another set of A outer beads. Pass needle through top 3 core beads from the bottom up (Fig. 3). Repeat three times. On fourth repetition, add B outer beads, referring to drawing (Fig. 4). On fifth repetition, add C outer beads (Fig. 5). Repeat this step five times in all.

❸Weave more four patterns (instructions in Step ② = one pattern).

❹Add a core bead and 8 2-mm seed beads. Pass needle through dual ring on strap finding. Pass needle through beads once more to form a loop. Finish off thread, making half-hitch knots as you go along. Remove stopper bead. Add 1 core bead and 8 2-mm seed beads. Attach to dual ring on strap finding. Finish off thread.

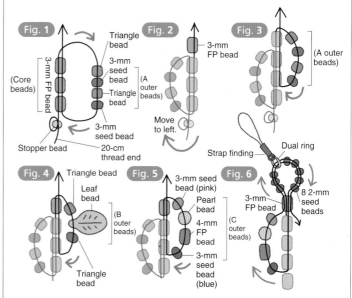

BRACELETS

We used several different stitches to make the pieces in this section. Some of them were introduced in previous sections (the spiral rope stitch, for instance). Others are appearing for the first time: (1) netting, a lacy stitch with open spaces between the beads, (2) the daisy chain stitch, which forms a continuous pattern resembling a daisy chain, (3) the right-angle weave stitch, which involves making a series of figure eights, and (4) the herringbone stitch, which has a chevron pattern. Some of the bracelets might be a bit difficult for beginners, but we urge you to pick the one you like best and rise to the challenge.

Spiral Rope Bracelet

Design: Kanai Yoko

We unified this sophisticated piece by using only white beads (3-mm seed beads for the core beads, and 2-mm seed beads and bugle beads for the outer beads). This bracelet has real presence, but isn't heavy-looking. It would look beautiful with a matching necklace.

Instructions: p.56
Spiral rope stitch
80 minutes

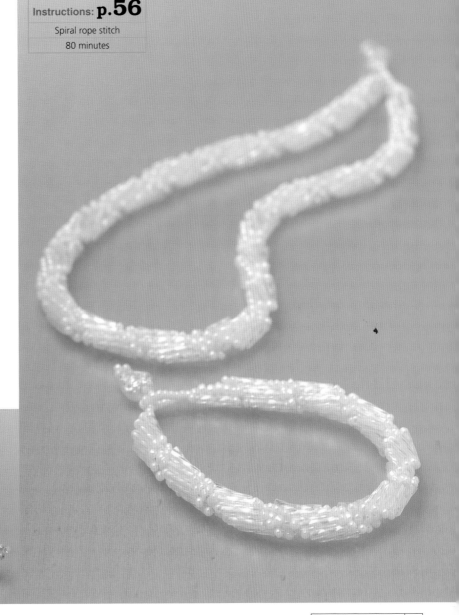

Instructions: **p.57**

Spiral rope stitch

80 minutes

Magatama Bead Spiral Bracelet

Design: Hiroka

This bracelet, with its smooth,
silky look, features magatama and
glass pearl beads. For a totally
different impression, use the
same types of beads, but
substitute bright or dark colors.

Instructions: **p.54**

Herringbone stitch

120 minutes

Lampwork Bead Bracelet

Design: Yoshida Akemi

The focal point of this bracelet is the lampwork beads at its center. The flexible herringbone-stitch tube is made with beads in three coordinating colors.

Instructions: **p.58**

Spiral rope stitch

60 minutes

Left: **Daisy Watch**
(for reference only)

Right: **Amethyst Spiral Watch**

Design: Sato Akemi

We love the elegant look of bracelet-style beaded watchbands. The watch at right is made using the spiral rope stitch. The outer beads are gemstone (amethyst) beads, which are combined intricately with Swarovski crystal beads. The watchband at left also incorporates gemstone beads (rhodonite and rhodocrosite) and crystal beads woven in the daisy chain stitch.

Bijoux Bracelet

Design: Miki Yuka

This connected figure-eight pattern in this bracelet is woven in right-angle weave stitch with 3-mm seed beads. We positioned pearl and fire-polished beads inside the stitches for an opulent but natural look.

Instructions: p.48

Netting

120 minutes

Netted Bracelet

Design: Hasumi Mayuko

Netting with bugle beads is ideal for beginners, because the work goes very quickly. Because netting is openwork, this bracelet is very light in weight and comfortable to wear. The fire-polished beads make gorgeous accents.

Instructions: p.59

Right-angle weave stitch

120 minutes

Instructions: **p.60**

Netting

150 minutes

Romantica Bracelet

Design: Yashiki Satoko

This lovely bracelet features brick-stitch triangles that open up into netting of sparkling three-cut beads. Since the spaces in the netting are fairly large, the bracelet opens up to envelop your arm. We chose colors that would produce a classic image for both versions of the bracelet.

Olive Bracelet

Design: Yokota Kyoko

This design was inspired by an olive grove in early summer, when the tiny flowers are just beginning to bloom. The stitch used is right-angle weave, which has a squared look in this bracelet because bugle beads are used instead of round ones.

Instructions: p.52

Right-angle weave stitch

52 minutes

(For reference only)

Herringbone stitch

Garland Bracelet

Design: Shudo Kimie

This bracelet is formed from a narrow herringbone-stitch cylinder adorned here and there with flower garlands. A lot of colors were used to make this bracelet, but the hues are muted for a feminine effect.

Instructions: **p.61**

Daisy chain stitch

60 minutes

Three-Strand Flower Bracelet

Design: Hasegawa Reiko

Like the bracelet shown at right, this one is made with the daisy chain stitch, but it has a more casual, whimsical look due to the twisted hex and leaf beads. The three strands give the bracelet mass. You could braid or twist the strands together to create a different effect.

Instructions: **p.50**

Daisy chain stitch

80 minutes

Daisy Chain Bracelet

Design: Uchida Kumiko

This design evokes wildflowers scattered over a meadow. The flowers, woven with fire-polished and pearl beads, and the seed-bead leaves are beautiful and refreshing.

Netted Bracelet

(Also shown on p. 44)

■Finished measurements:

2.5cm W x 18cm L (netting: 15.5cm L)

■Supplies

· 2.3m beading thread (see p. 74)
· 55 3-mm round fire-polished beads (red jasper) #α6603-55
· 56 6-mm bugle beads (cream) #123
· 367 2-mm seed beads (gunmetal) #989
· 55 1.5-mm seed beads (gold) #557
· 8-mm round lampwork bead red) #α5820

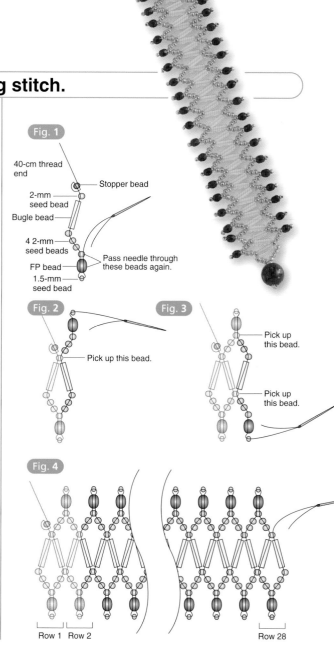

1 Weave bracelet, using the netting stitch.

❶String a stopper bead on thread, leaving a 40-cm end. Add a 2-mm seed bead, a bugle bead, 4 more 2-mm seed beads, a fire-polished bead and a 1.5-mm seed bead. Pass needle back through a fire-polished bead and a 2-mm seed bead (Fig. 1).

❷Add 3 2-mm seed beads and a bugle bead. Pick up first 2-mm seed bead strung in Step ①. Add 3 more 2-mm seed beads, a fire-polished bead and a 1.5-mm seed bead (Fig. 2).

❸Pick up a fire-polished bead and a 2-mm seed bead. Add 3 2-mm seed beads and a bugle bead. Pick up 2-mm seed bead indicated in drawing. Add 3 2-mm seed beads, a fire-polished bead and 2 1.5-mm seed beads (Fig. 3).

❹Repeat Step ③ until you have 27 rows of netting. On Row 28, pick up fire-polished and 2-mm seed beads. Then string 3 2-mm seed beads and a bugle bead on thread and pick up a 2-mm seed bead (Fig. 4).

Fig. 1

40-cm thread end

Stopper bead

2-mm seed bead

Bugle bead

4 2-mm seed beads

Pass needle through these beads again.

FP bead

1.5-mm seed bead

Fig. 2

Pick up this bead.

Fig. 3

Pick up this bead.

Pick up this bead.

Fig. 4

Row 1 Row 2

Row 28

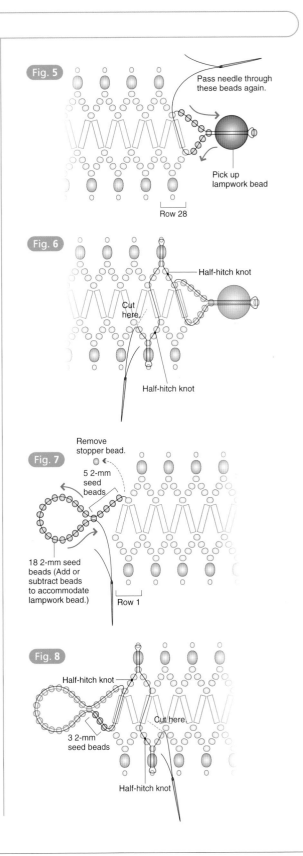

② Make clasp.

❶ Add 5 2-mm seed beads, lampwork bead and one more 2-mm seed bead. Pass needle back through lampwork bead and a 2-mm seed bead, referring to drawing. Add 3 2-mm seed beads, then pick up a 2-mm seed bead, a bugle bead and one more 2-mm seed bead, as indicated in drawing (Fig. 5).

❷ Pass needle through beads in clasp once again for added strength. Run needle through beads in netting, making half-hitch knots 2-3 times as you go along. Cut excess thread at edge of a bead (Fig. 6).

❸ Remove stopper bead. String 5 2-mm seed beads on thread end left at beginning of work. Add 18 more 2-mm seed beads and pick up 5th 2-mm seed bead on clasp loop. Make sure lampwork bead fits inside loop. Add or subtract 2-mm seed beads if necessary (Fig. 7).

❹ String 3 2-mm seed beads and pick up a 2-mm seed bead, a bugle bead and another 2-mm seed bead, as indicated in drawing. Pass thread through clasp loop once again for added strength. Finish off thread as in Step ② (Fig. 8).

Fig. 5

Pass needle through these beads again.

Pick up lampwork bead

Row 28

Fig. 6

Half-hitch knot

Cut here

Half-hitch knot

Fig. 7

Remove stopper bead.

5 2-mm seed beads

18 2-mm seed beads (Add or subtract beads to accommodate lampwork bead.)

Row 1

Fig. 8

Half-hitch knot

Cut here.

3 2-mm seed beads

Half-hitch knot

Daisy Chain Bracelet

(Also shown on p. 47)

■Finished length:

15cm (excluding clasp)

■Supplies

· 1.5m beading thread (see p. 74)
· 6 4-mm round glass pearl beads (pink) #α387-5
· 36 3-mm round fire-polished beads (CAL pink) #α6603-82
· 67 2-mm seed beads (bronze) #221
· 84 2-mm seed beads (green) #242
· 70 2-mm seed beads (dark green) #243
· 21 3-mm seed beads (dark rose) #356
· Hook-and-eye clasp (antique gold) #α4221GF

*See p. 62 for supplies for white bracelet.

1 Weave bracelet, using the daisy chain stitch.

❶String 4 bronze seed beads, the eye of the clasp and 3 more bronze seed beads on thread, leaving a 20-cm end. Run needle back through beads in loop just formed and tie a square knot (Fig. 1).

❷Pick up first seed bead strung, then add 6 bronze and 6 dark green seed beads (Fig. 2).

❸Pick up 5th dark green 2-mm seed bead from the opposite direction. Add 4 dark green seed beads, and pick up 6th bronze 2-mm seed bead strung in Step ②. You have woven one leaf (Fig. 3).

❹String 3 bronze 2-mm seed beads and 6 fire-polished beads (Fig. 4).

❺Pick up first fire-polished bead, working in the same direction, to form a circle. String a pearl bead and pick up 4th fire-polished bead, working in opposite direction. You have woven one daisy (Fig. 5).

❻Make 7 leaves and 6 daisies, alternating between the two and separating each leaf and daisy with 3 bronze seed beads (Fig. 6).

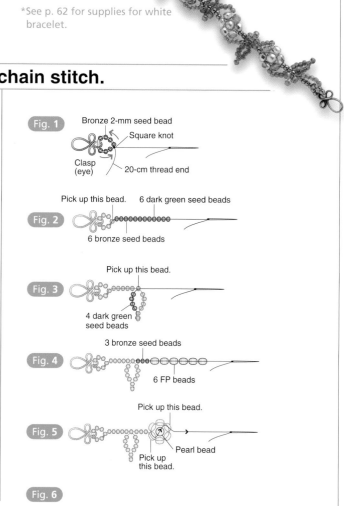

Fig. 1
Bronze 2-mm seed bead
Square knot
Clasp (eye)
20-cm thread end

Fig. 2
Pick up this bead.
6 dark green seed beads
6 bronze seed beads

Fig. 3
Pick up this bead.
4 dark green seed beads

Fig. 4
3 bronze seed beads
6 FP beads

Fig. 5
Pick up this bead.
Pearl bead
Pick up this bead.

Fig. 6

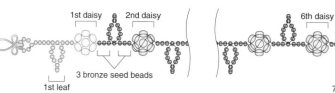

1st daisy   2nd daisy   6th daisy
3 bronze seed beads
1st leaf   7th leaf

❼Add 9 bronze seed beads, hook half of clasp and 3 more bronze seed beads (Fig. 7).

❽Pick up 6th bronze seed bead, working in same direction, to close circle. Pass needle through beads in loop again for added strength (Fig. 8).

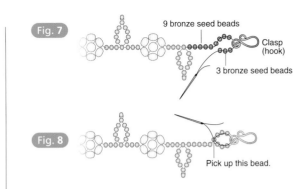

Fig. 7

9 bronze seed beads

Clasp (hook)

3 bronze seed beads

Fig. 8

Pick up this bead.

② Decorate daisy chain.

❶String 5 green seed beads on thread. Pick up bronze seed bead from base of leaf (Fig. 9).

❷Add 3 3-mm seed beads, then pick up same bronze 2-mm seed bead at base of leaf, working in same direction (Fig. 10).

❸String 5 green seed beads. Pick up 3 fire-polished beads in daisy, as shown in drawing (Fig. 11).

❹Repeat Steps ① - ③ until you reach other end of bracelet (beginning of work). Pick up first bronze seed bead strung in 1 ① (Fig. 12).

❺Run thread through beads indicated in drawing, making 2-3 half-hitch knots as you go along. Cut excess thread at the edge of a bead (Fig. 13).

❻Run needle with thread end left at beginning of work through beads indicated in drawing. Finish off thread as directed in Step ⑤ (Fig. 14).

Fig. 9

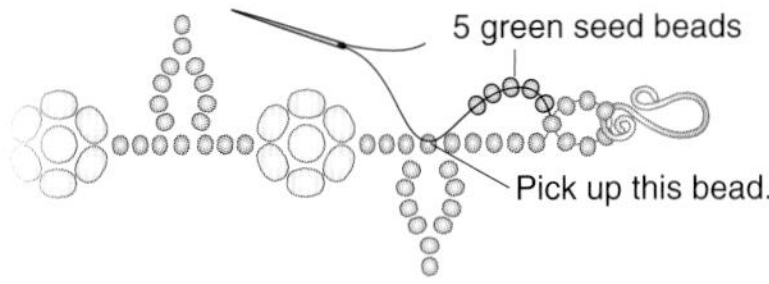

5 green seed beads

Pick up this bead.

Fig. 10

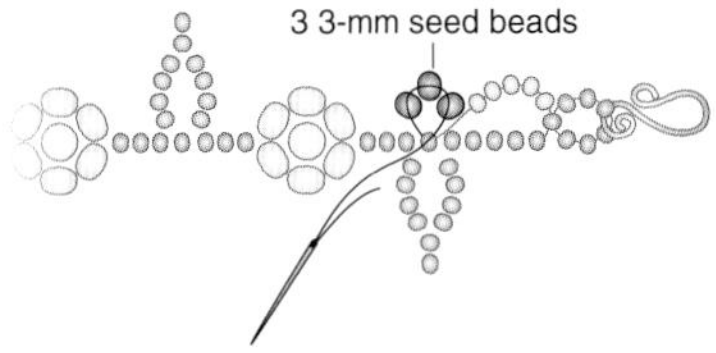

3 3-mm seed beads

Fig. 11

5 green seed beads

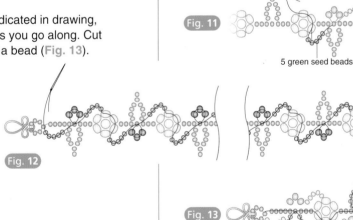

Fig. 12

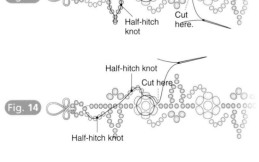

Fig. 13

Half-hitch knot

Half-hitch knot

Cut here.

Fig. 14

Half-hitch knot

Cut here

Half-hitch knot

Olive Bracelet

(Also shown on p. 46)

■Finished measurements:

1.3cm W x 6cm L

■Supplies

· 2.5m beading thread (see p. 74)
· 64 6-mm bugle beads (pale green) #172
· 2 3-mm round fire-polished beads (opal) #α6603-51
· 42 4-mm round fire-polished beads (opal) #α6604-51
· 166 2-mm seed beads (dark green) #324
· 13-mm cube faceted acrylic bead (olive) #PB754

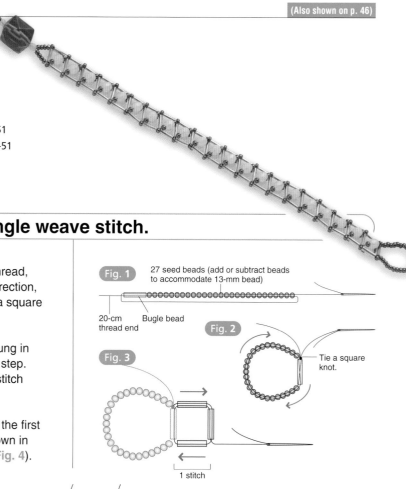

1 Make bracelet in right-angle weave stitch.

❶String a bugle bead and 27 seed beads on thread, leaving a 20-cm end. Working in the same direction, pick up all these beads. Pull threads and tie a square knot (Figs. 1, 2).

❷String 3 bugle beads. Pick up bugle bead strung in Step ① and first 2 bugle beads added in this step. You have completed one right-angle weave stitch (Fig. 3).

❸String 3 bugle beads. Pick up one bead from the first stitch, and two from the second stitch, as shown in drawing. Repeat until you have 21 stitches (Fig. 4).

Fig. 1
27 seed beads (add or subtract beads to accommodate 13-mm bead)

20-cm thread end   Bugle bead

Fig. 2
Tie a square knot.

Fig. 3

1 stitch

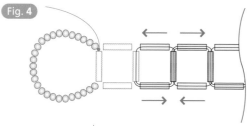

Fig. 4

21 stitches

❹Make clasp: string 4 seed beads, a 3-mm fire-polished bead, the 13-mm cube bead, another 3-mm fire-polished bead and 3 more seed beads on same thread. Pass needle back through beads, as shown in drawing. Add 4 more seed beads (Fig. 5).

❺Pick up bugle bead in 21st stitch to close loop. Pass needle through beads in clasp once again for added strength (Fig. 6).

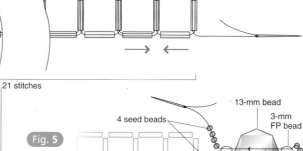

Fig. 5
4 seed beads
13-mm bead
3-mm FP bead
3 seed beads

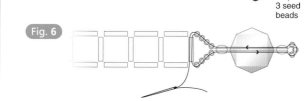

Fig. 6

② Decorate bracelet.

❶ String a seed bead, a 4-mm fire-polished bead and another seed bead. Pick up bugle bead indicated in drawing (Fig. 7).

❷ Again, add a seed bead, a 4-mm fire-polished bead and another seed bead. Pick up a bugle bead as in Step ①. Repeat until you reach other end of bracelet (Fig. 8).

❸ Turn bracelet over and pick up bugle bead indicated in drawing (Fig. 9).

❹ Add a seed bead, a 4-mm fire-polished bead and another seed bead. Pick up a bugle bead, as on other side of bracelet. Repeat until you reach other end of bracelet (beginning of work). The beads should be facing the same way on both sides (Fig. 10).

❺ String a seed bead on thread extending from bugle bead on right side of bracelet. Pick up a bugle bead on outer edge. Repeat, adding one seed bead at a time and picking up a bugle bead, until you reach other end of bracelet (Fig. 11).

❻ Pass needle with thread from end of work through beads, as indicated in drawing, tying half-hitch knots 2-3 times as you go along. Cut excess thread at edge of a bead (Fig. 12).

❼ Finish off thread end at beginning of work as in Step ⑥.

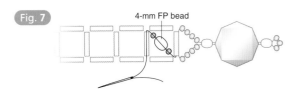

Fig. 7 — 4-mm FP bead

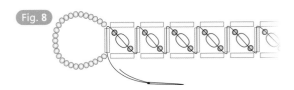

Fig. 8

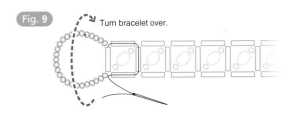

Fig. 9 — Turn bracelet over.

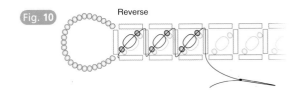

Fig. 10 — Reverse

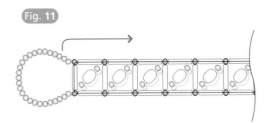

Fig. 11

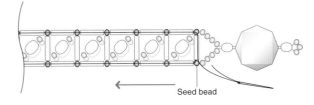

Seed bead

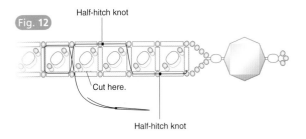

Fig. 12 — Half-hitch knot — Cut here. — Half-hitch knot

Lampwork Bead Bracelet

(Also shown on p. 43)

■Finished length:

17cm (woven portion: 7cm)

■Supplies

· 4.5m beading thread (see p. 74)
· 100 2.2-mm triangle beads (light gold) #262
· 100 2.2-mm triangle beads (reddish gold) #278
· 100 2.2-mm triangle beads (matte light blue-green) #721
· 2 4-mm round fire-polished beads (aquamarine) #α6604-106
· 12 6-mm round fire-polished beads (aquamarine) #α6606-106
· 10-mm round lampwork bead (blue-green) #α1995
· 21 1.5-mm seed beads (light gold) #262
· Snap clasp set (silver) #9-1-3S

1 Weave two herringbone-stitch tubes.

❶Round 1 is worked in ladder stitch. Cut a 2-m length of thread. String 2 light blue-green (hereafter, blue-green) triangle beads on thread, leaving a 30-cm end. Pass thread through both beads, working in the same direction. Pull threads so that beads are positioned next to each other, as shown in drawing (Fig. 1).

❷String a light gold triangle bead. Pick up 2nd blue-green triangle bead strung and light gold triangle bead, referring to drawing (Fig. 2).

❸String a light gold triangle bead, then pick up 3rd and 4th light gold triangle beads. Repeat, using colors indicated in drawings (Fig. 3).

❹Pick up first blue-green triangle bead to close circle. Then pick up 6th and first triangle bead, and begin Round 2 (Fig. 4).

❺Begin working in herringbone stitch. String 2 blue-green triangle beads, then pick up 2 blue-green beads from the previous round from above (Fig. 5).

❻Pick up third light gold triangle bead from previous round, from below (Fig. 6).

❼Working as in Steps ❺ and ❻, add triangle beads of the same color as those in the preceding round (Fig. 7).

❽After completing round, pick up first blue-green triangle beads in Rounds 1 and 2, and begin Round 3 (Fig. 8).

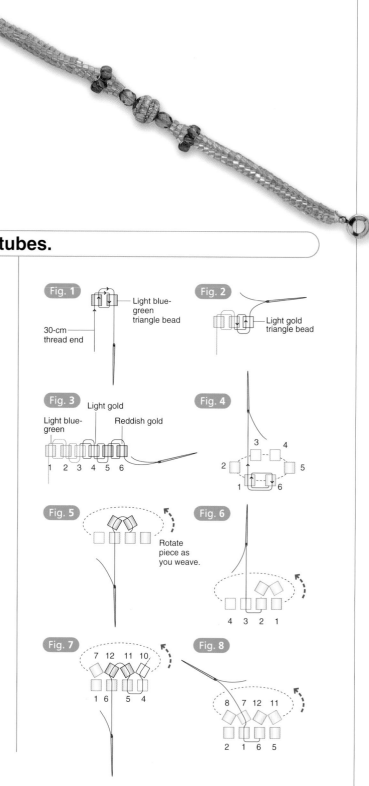

❾ In Round 3 and thereafter, continue picking up beads from previous row, referring to drawing (Fig. 9).

❿ When you have completed that round, pick up 2 blue-green triangle beads and begin next round (Fig. 10).

⓫ When you have woven 22 rounds with triangle beads, weave Round 23 with 4-mm fire-polished beads, and Rounds 24 and 25 with triangle beads once again (Fig. 11).

⓬ Work Round 26 (last row) in ladder stitch, the same as Round 1, but begin by working as you did for the herringbone stitch (Fig. 12).

⓭ Work ladder stitch as in Round 1. Set aside thread at end of work. You now have a herringbone-stitch tube (Fig. 13).

⓮ Make another tube, changing the colors of the triangle beads as indicated, and using the remaining thread. After Round 2, add beads of the same color as those in the previous round (Fig. 14).

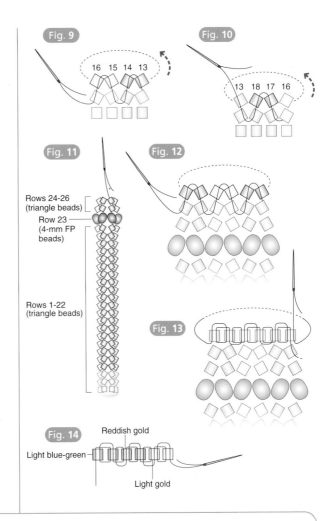

Fig. 9   Fig. 10

Fig. 11   Fig. 12

Rows 24-26 (triangle beads)
Row 23 (4-mm FP beads)

Rows 1-22 (triangle beads)

Fig. 13

Fig. 14
Reddish gold
Light blue-green
Light gold

② **Assemble bracelet.**

❶ String a 6-mm fire-polished bead, lampwork bead and another 6-mm fire-polished bead on thread extending from end of tube (Fig. 15).

❷ Pick up beads from other tube, as shown in drawing. Then return to first tube, picking up fire-polished bead, lampwork bead and another fire-polished bead and making half-hitch knots 2-3 times as you go along. Pass needle with thread extending from end of other tube through fire-polished and lampwork beads in the same way (Fig. 16).

❸ String 5 1.5-mm seed beads, socket of snap clasp and 5 more 1.5-mm seed beads on thread end at beginning of work. Pick up beads as indicated in drawing, going around piece twice. Finish off thread, making half-hitch knots as you go (Fig. 17).

❹ String 11 1.5-mm seed beads and ball half of clasp on thread end at beginning of other tube. Go around piece twice, as in Step ③. Finish off thread (Fig. 18).

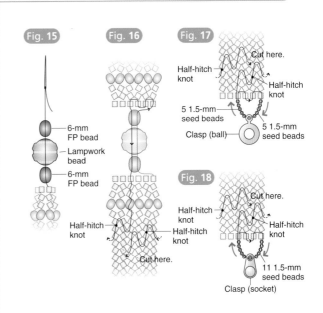

Fig. 15   Fig. 16   Fig. 17

Cut here.
Half-hitch knot
Half-hitch knot
5 1.5-mm seed beads
5 1.5-mm seed beads
Clasp (ball)

6-mm FP bead
Lampwork bead
6-mm FP bead

Half-hitch knot
Half-hitch knot
Half-hitch knot
Cut here.

Fig. 18
Cut here.
Half-hitch knot
Half-hitch knot
Half-hitch knot
11 1.5-mm seed beads
Clasp (socket)

Spiral Rope Bracelet

(Also shown on p. 41)

■Finished length:

20cm (woven portion: 17cm)

■Supplies

· 3.2m beading thread (see p. 74)
· 90 3-mm seed beads (white) #121
· 195 2-mm seed beads (white) #121
· 85 9-mm twisted hex beads (aurora) #161
· 8 x 11-mm lampwork bead with silver foil #α 1978

*See p. 62 for supplies for white-and-gold bracelet.

❶String a stopper bead on thread, leaving a 30-cm end. String 6 3-mm seed beads (core beads) and one 2-mm seed bead, one twisted hex bead and another 2-mm seed bead (outer beads). Pass needle through core beads again (Fig. 1).

❷String another core bead. Move outer beads around to left (Fig. 2).

❸String another set of outer beads, as in Step ①. Pick up 6 core beads from above (Fig. 3). Repeat until you have 85 spirals.

❹Make clasp, using same thread: string 6 2-mm seed beads, lampwork bead and 3 more 2-mm seed beads. Pass needle back through lampwork bead and 6 2-mm seed beads. Pick up beads indicated in drawing again for added strength. Finish off thread, making half-hitch knots as you go along (Fig. 4).

❺Remove stopper bead at beginning of work. String 16 2-mm seed beads and form a loop. Pass needle through beads in loop again. Finish off thread, making half-hitch knots as you go along (Fig. 5).

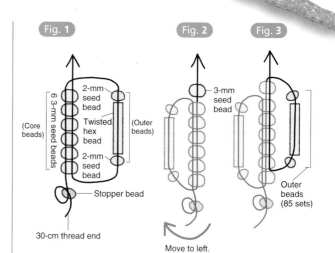

Fig. 1

6 3-mm seed beads
(Core beads)
2-mm seed bead
Twisted hex bead
(Outer beads)
2-mm seed bead
Stopper bead
30-cm thread end

Fig. 2

3-mm seed bead
Move to left.

Fig. 3

Outer beads (85 sets)

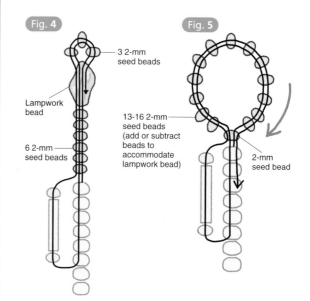

Fig. 4

3 2-mm seed beads
Lampwork bead
6 2-mm seed beads

Fig. 5

13-16 2-mm seed beads (add or subtract beads to accommodate lampwork bead)
2-mm seed bead

Variation: Necklace

■Finished length:

42cm (woven portion: 39cm)

■Supplies

· 7m beading thread (see p. 74)
· 212 3-mm seed beads (white) #121
· 439 2-mm seed beads (white) #121
· 207 9-mm twisted hex beads (aurora) #161
· 8 x 11-mm lampwork bead with silver foil #α 1978

Magatama Bead Spiral Bracelet

(Also shown on p. 41)

■Finished length:

18cm (woven portion: 16cm)

■Supplies

· 2m beading thread (see p. 74)
· 120 4-mm magatama beads (brown) #M0202
· 63 3-mm hex beads (gold-lined translucent) #22
· 60 4-mm glass pearl beads (beige) #α387-14
· 140 2-mm seed beads (gold-lined gunmetal) #262
· Snap clasp (gold) #9-1-9G

*See p. 62 for supplies for lavender and gray bracelets.

❶String a stopper bead on thread, leaving a 30-cm end. String 4 hex beads (core beads) and 2-mm seed beads, magatama beads and pearl bead (outer beads) as shown in drawing. Pass needle through the 4 core beads again (Fig. 1).

❷Add another core bead. Move outer beads around to left (Fig. 2).

❸String another set of outer beads, as in Step ①. Pick up 4 core beads from above (Fig. 3). Repeat until you have 60 sets of outer beads.

❹On same thread string 5 2-mm seed beads, ring on socket of clasp and 5 more 2-mm seed beads, forming a loop. Pass needle back through beads indicated in drawing for added strength. Finish off thread, making half-hitch knots as you go along (Fig. 4).

❺Remove stopper bead at beginning of work. String seed beads and ring on ball of clasp, forming a loop as in Step ④. Pass needle through beads in loop again. Finish off thread, making half-hitch knots as you go along (Fig. 5).

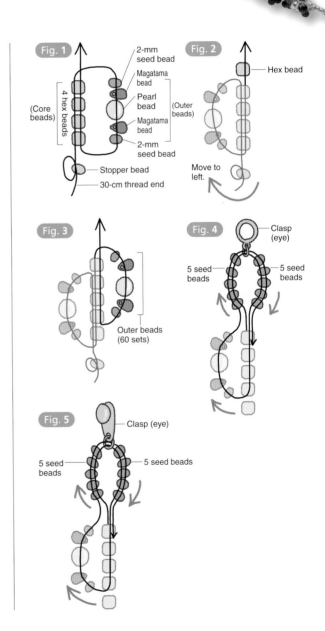

Fig. 1 · 2-mm seed bead · Magatama bead · Pearl bead · Magatama bead · 2-mm seed bead · (Core beads) · 4 hex beads · (Outer beads) · Stopper bead · 30-cm thread end

Fig. 2 · Hex bead · Move to left.

Fig. 3 · Outer beads (60 sets)

Fig. 4 · Clasp (eye) · 5 seed beads · 5 seed beads

Fig. 5 · Clasp (eye) · 5 seed beads · 5 seed beads

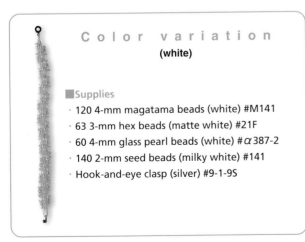

    C o l o r   v a r i a t i o n
             (white)

■Supplies

· 120 4-mm magatama beads (white) #M141
· 63 3-mm hex beads (matte white) #21F
· 60 4-mm glass pearl beads (white) #α387-2
· 140 2-mm seed beads (milky white) #141
· Hook-and-eye clasp (silver) #9-1-9S

Amethyst Spiral Watch

(Also shown on p. 43)

■Finished length:

18cm (woven portion: 13.5cm)

■Supplies

· 1.5m beading thread (see p. 74)
· 24 4-mm Swarovski bicone crystal beads (tanzanite) #13
· 17 amethyst chip beads #α1523
· 186 Aiko beads (lavender) #202
· 62 3-mm seed beads (bronze) #221
· 21-mm round watch face (antique gold)
· 13.5cm elongated cable chain (antique gold) #α668GF
· 12 0.5 x 22-mm headpins (antique gold) #α624GF
· 4 4.5-mm jump rings (antique gold) #α4253GF
· Bar-and-ring toggle clasp (antique gold) #α4227GF

❶String a stopper bead on thread, leaving a 25-cm end. String 5 seed beads (core beads), then Pattern A outer beads (3 Aiko beads, one crystal bead and 3 more Aiko beads, as shown in drawing. Pass needle through the 5 core beads again (Fig. 1).

❷String 2 more core beads. Move outer beads around to left (Fig. 2).

❸String Pattern B outer beads (3 Aiko beads, a chip bead and 3 more Aiko beads). Pick up 5 core beads from above (Fig. 3). Repeat, alternating Patterns A and B until you have 29 sets of outer beads.

❹String watch face on same thread: add 3 Aiko beads, ring extending from bottom of watch face and 3 more Aiko beads, forming a loop. Pass needle back through beads as indicated in drawing for added strength. Finish off thread, making half-hitch knots as you go along (Fig. 4).

❺Remove stopper bead at beginning of work. String Aiko beads and bar of clasp, forming a loop, as in Step ④. Pass needle through beads in loop again. Finish off thread, making half-hitch knots as you go along (Fig. 5).

❻Attach watch face to ring of clasp with a jump ring (Fig. 6).

❼Make 9 components with a headpin and a crystal bead, and 3 components with a headpin and a chip bead. Attach 7 of the crystal-bead components to the chain at regular intervals. Attach one end of chain to bead loop on bar of clasp with 2 jump rings. Attach other end of chain to ring on bottom of watch face with a jump ring. Attach 2 chip-bead components to same jump ring (Fig. 7).

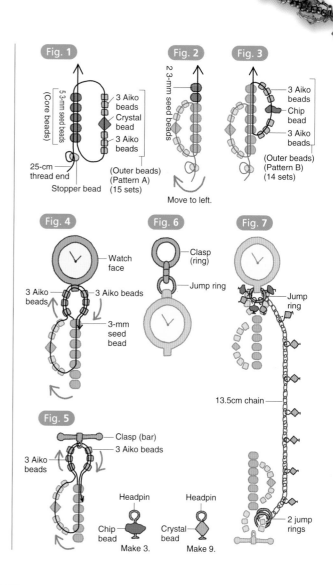

Fig. 1
5 3-mm seed beads (Core beads)
3 Aiko beads
Crystal bead
3 Aiko beads
25-cm thread end
Stopper bead
(Outer beads) (Pattern A) (15 sets)

Fig. 2
2 3-mm seed beads
Move to left.

Fig. 3
3 Aiko beads
Chip bead
3 Aiko beads
(Outer beads) (Pattern B) (14 sets)

Fig. 4
Watch face
3 Aiko beads
3 Aiko beads
3-mm seed bead

Fig. 6
Clasp (ring)
Jump ring
Watch face

Fig. 7
Jump ring
13.5cm chain
2 jump rings

Fig. 5
Clasp (bar)
3 Aiko beads
3 Aiko beads
Headpin
Headpin
Chip bead
Make 3.
Crystal bead
Make 9.

Bijoux Bracelet

(Also shown on p. 44)

■Finished length:

18cm (woven portion: 14.5cm)

■Supplies

· 5m beading thread (see p. 74)
· 13 4-mm round fire-polished beads (antique brass) #α6604-42
· 9 5-mm round fire-polished beads (topaz) #α6605-18
· 14 6-mm round glass pearl beads (beige) #α388-14
· 120 2-mm seed beads (dark bronze) #222
· 276 3-mm seed beads (bronze) #221
· 20-mm disc shell bead with side hole (dark orange)

❶String a stopper bead on center of 5m thread. Wrap other end around a piece of cardboard. String 12 3-mm seed beads. Pick up 9th bead, counting from the beginning and working in the same direction. Pull thread (Figs. 1 and 2).

❷String 9 3-mm seed beads. Pass needle through last 3 beads in first stitch and first 6 beads from 2nd stitch. Make 18 right-angle weave stitches in the same way. On 18th stitch, make transition to Row 2 by picking up first 9 beads (Fig. 3).

❸For first stitch in Row 2, string 9 3-mm seed beads. Pick up last 3 beads in Row 1 and first 3 beads in Row 2. Starting with the 2nd stitch, string 6 3-mm seed beads and pick up 3 beads from Row 1, as shown in drawing (Fig. 4). Finish off thread, running needle back through beads and making half-hitch knots as you go.

❹Turn piece over and decorate Row 1. Remove stopper bead, and on thread end left at beginning of work, string a 2-mm seed bead, a pearl bead and another 2-mm seed bead. Then pick up 3 3-mm seed beads indicated in drawing. Working in the same way, add 2 2-mm seed beads and a 6-mm fire-polished bead, or 4 2-mm seed beads and a 4-mm fire-polished bead, at locations of your choice. On 18th stitch, pick up 3-mm seed beads and bring needle out where shown in drawing (Fig. 5).

❺Attach clasp: string 5 2-mm seed beads, shell bead and 5 more 2-mm seed beads. Pick up beads indicated in drawing for added strength (Fig. 6).

❻Decorate Row 2: picking up 3-mm seed beads indicated in drawing, add beads as in Step ④ (Fig. 7).

❼Make loop of clasp by stringing 30 2-mm seed beads on thread extending from Row 1. Run needle through beads in loop twice more. Pick up 3-mm seed beads indicated in drawing. Run needle through those beads again for added strength. Run needle through beads in woven piece and finish off thread (Fig. 8).

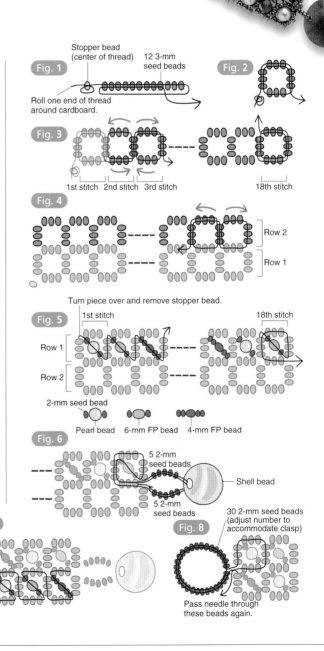

Fig. 1
Stopper bead (center of thread)
12 3-mm seed beads
Roll one end of thread around cardboard.

Fig. 2

Fig. 3
1st stitch 2nd stitch 3rd stitch
18th stitch

Fig. 4
Row 2
Row 1

Turn piece over and remove stopper bead.

Fig. 5
1st stitch
18th stitch
Row 1
Row 2
2-mm seed bead
Pearl bead   6-mm FP bead   4-mm FP bead

Fig. 6
5 2-mm seed beads
Shell bead
5 2-mm seed beads

Fig. 7

Fig. 8
30 2-mm seed beads (adjust number to accommodate clasp)
Pass needle through these beads again.

Romantica bracelet

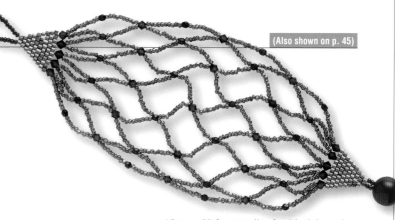

(Also shown on p. 45)

■**Finished length:**

20cm (netting: 13.5cm)

■**Supplies**

· 3.2m beading thread (see p. 74)
· 25 4-mm Swarovski bicone crystal beads (b
· 24 3-mm round fire-polished beads (dark r
· 30 2-mm seed beads (dark red) #5D
· 720 2-mm 3-cut beads (dark pink) #CR177
· 108 2-mm hex beads (reddish bronze) #222
· 12-mm round acrylic bead (red agate) #J502

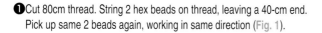

*See p. 62 for supplies for black bracelet.

❶ Cut 80cm thread. String 2 hex beads on thread, leaving a 40-cm end. Pick up same 2 beads again, working in same direction (Fig. 1).

❷ Weave Row 2: string 2 hex beads, and pick up working thread in Row 1 from the back. Then pick up 2nd hex bead from underneath. String another hex bead, and pick up working thread from previous row once again. Pick up last hex bead from underneath (Fig. 2: brick stitch).

❸ In Row 3 and subsequent rows, work as in Step ②, stringing a hex bead and picking up working thread in previous row, as indicated in drawing. Make a one-bead increase at left and right edge of every row until you have 9 rows (Figs. 3 and 4). Run needle diagonally through beads, turning to form intersections once or twice. Cut excess thread. Do not finish off thread at beginning of work.

❹ Make another identical motif, as in Step ③, with remaining thread. Set 40-cm thread end at beginning of work aside for now.

❺ Weave netting, using same thread: string a crystal bead, 9 3-cut beads, a fire-polished bead and 9 more 3-cut beads. Repeat, referring to drawing. After stringing the last crystal bead, pick up 2 hex beads from triangular motif. Turn; working backwards, string 9 3-cut beads at a time and pick up crystal and fire-polished beads as you go along. Continue stringing beads as indicated in drawing. Pass needle through beads in netting and finish off thread (Fig. 5).

❻ String 23 seed beads on thread end left at beginning of work, forming a loop. Pick up hex beads in triangular motif and run needle through beads in loop again. Finish off thread (Fig. 6).

❼ Make clasp: string 2 seed beads, acrylic bead and 3 more seed beads on thread at other end of bracelet. Pass needle through acrylic bead again and add 2 more seed beads. Pick up hex beads in triangular motif. Pass needle through clasp beads again and finish off thread as in Step ⑥ (Fig. 7).

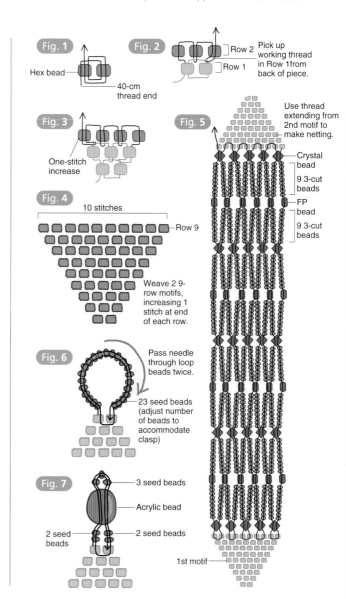

Three-Strand Flower Bracelet

(Also shown on p. 47)

■Finished length:

21cm (woven portion: 18cm)

■Supplies

· 1.5m beading thread (see p. 74)
· 36 9-mm twisted hex beads (green) #707
· 15 4-mm round glass pearl beads (yellow-green) #α387-13
· 12 4-mm round fire-polished beads (CAL orange) #α6604-87
· 230 2-mm seed beads (yellow) #302
· 15 7 x 12-mm pressed-glass leaf beads (gold-lined yellow-green)
· Flower bar-and-ring toggle clasp (antique gold) #α4233GF

*See p. 62 for supplies for pink bracelet.

❶String a stopper bead on thread, leaving a 20-cm end. Then string beads for Pattern A (a twisted hex bead, a fire-polished bead and another twisted hex bead), Pattern B (a leaf bead, 12 seed beads and a pearl bead (one daisy-chain stitch), a twisted hex bead, 5 seed beads and a twisted hex bead), Pattern C (a leaf bead, 12 seed beads and a pearl bead (one daisy-chain stitch), a twisted hex bead, a fire-polished bead and another twisted hex bead). Repeat, referring to Fig. 2 for order. Add a seed bead after the 3rd, 6th and last repetition of Pattern C and change directions as shown in drawings (Figs. 1 and 2).

❷With same thread, pick up seed bead between first and 2nd strands. Add 6 seed beads, bar of clasp and 6 more seed beads, forming a loop. Pass needle back through loop beads for added strength, then through beads in bracelet to finish off thread, making half-hitch knots as you go (Fig. 3).

❸Remove stopper bead. String a seed bead on thread at beginning of work. Pick up seed bead between 2nd and 3rd strands. Then add 2 seed beads, ring of clasp and 2 more seed beads, forming a loop. Pass needle through beads in loop again. Finish off thread by passing needle through beads in bracelet, making half-hitch knots as you go (Fig. 4).

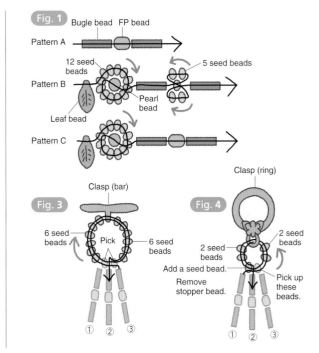

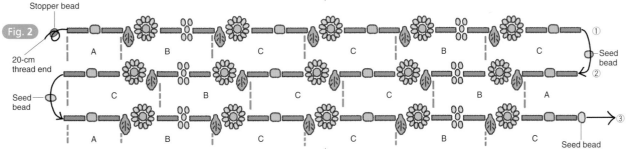

Supplies for color variations
(Please refer to main instructions for thread amounts.)

Daisy Chain Bracelet (white)

Instructions p. 50

- 6 4-mm round glass pearl beads (white) #α387-2
- 36 3-mm round fire-polished beads (silver crystal) #α6603-29
- 67 2-mm seed beads (white) #777
- 84 2-mm seed beads (green) #242
- 70 2-mm seed beads (dark green) #243
- 21 3-mm seed beads (yellow-green) #164
- Hook-and-eye clasp (silver) #α4221S

Spiral Rope Bracelet (white/gold)

Instructions p. 56

- 90 3-mm seed beads (gold-plated) #751
- 195 2-mm seed beads (gold-plated) #751
- 85 9-mm twisted hex beads (gold-plated) #701
- 10-mm round lampwork bead (multi) #α1989

Magatama Bead Spiral Bracelet (lavender)

Instructions p. 57

- 120 4-mm magatama beads (pink aurora) #M171
- 63 3-mm hex beads (matte white) #21F
- 60 4-mm glass pearl beads (lavender) #α387-8
- 140 2-mm seed beads (light pink) #166
- Snap clasp (silver) #9-1-9S

Magatama Bead Spiral Bracelet (gray)

Instructions p. 57

- 120 4-mm magatama beads (black) #M0109
- 63 3-mm hex beads (matte white) #21F
- 60 4-mm glass pearl beads (dark gray) #α387-17
- 140 2-mm seed beads (light gray) #113
- Snap clasp (silver) #9-1-9S

Romantica Bracelet (black)

Instructions p. 60

- 108 2-mm hexagonal beads (dark green metallic) #83
- 24 3-mm round fire-polished beads (jet) #α6603-21
- 720 2-mm 3-cut beads (dark blue) #CR244
- 10 4-mm bicone Swarovski crystal beads (morion)
- 5 4-mm bicone Swarovski crystal beads (Indian sapphire)
- 10 4-mm bicone Swarovski crystal beads (erinite)
- 30 2-mm seed beads (metallic dark green) #83
- 10-mm round acrylic bead (black) #α354

Three-Strand Flower Bracelet (pink)

Instructions p. 61

- 36 9-mm twisted hex beads (purple) #615
- 15 4-mm round glass pearl beads (pink) #α387-6
- 12 4-mm round fire-polished beads (silver crystal) #α6604-29
- 230 2-mm seed beads (pink) #291
- 15 7 x 12-mm pressed-glass leaf beads (gold-lined pink)
- Flower bar-and-ring toggle clasp (silver) #α4233S

Short Herringbone-Stitch Lariat (gold)

Instructions p. 73

- 2,700 2-mm seed beads (gold) #701
- 40 4-mm magatama beads (gold-lined translucent) #M22
- 40 4-mm magatama beads (translucent) #M01
- 40 4-mm magatama beads (topaz) #M0102
- 12 4-mm round pearl beads (metallic gold) #301
- 12 6-mm round metal beads (gold) #7165

Short Herringbone-Stitch Lariat (silver)

Instructions p. 73

- 2,700 2-mm 3-cut beads (silver) #α714
- 40 4-mm magatama beads (translucent) #M01
- 40 4-mm magatama beads (silver-lined translucent) #M21
- 40 4-mm magatama beads (aurora) #M161
- 12 4-mm round glass pearl beads (pale moss green) #α387-13
- 12 5 x 6-mm oval glass pearl beads (pale moss green) #α389-13

Part 5

NECKLACES, CHOKERS AND LARIATS

Once you've gotten used to working with beads, needle and thread, you're probably ready to try making a necklace. Long necklaces and lariats will, of course, require more time and effort. But some of the pieces in this section are made by simply repeating the same steps over and over again, and you'll find that the work goes fast. All the stitches used to make these necklaces (spiral rope stitch, herringbone stitch and netting) have been introduced in previous sections. All these designs emphasize the beauty of the stitches used to make them. We're sure you'll want to make several of these necklaces.

Instructions: p.70
Spiral rope stitch
90 minutes

Instructions: p.70

Spiral Necklace in Autumn Colors

Design: Takemura Takako

In this luxurious design, seed beads in various shades of purple surround a line of glass pearl beads. Pulling gently on the thread is key to forming the graceful spiral. You could make one of these for each season, using example, shades of pink for spring, turquoise for summer and white for winter.

Instructions: **p.70**

Spiral rope stitch

120 minutes

Long Spiral Necklace

Design: Kozuma Emi

Black and silver beads are
combined to make this very
sophisticated necklace.
The simple design will enhance
any type of fashion, from casual
attire to evening wear. The beads
used are slightly on the large side,
so the work will go quickly, even
though the necklace is long.

Two-Way Heart Necklace

Design: Seki Keiko

In this delicate necklace, the spiral
ropes are accents. The fire-polished
and Swarovski crystal beads make a
statement without dominating.
Wear this as a necklace or a lariat.

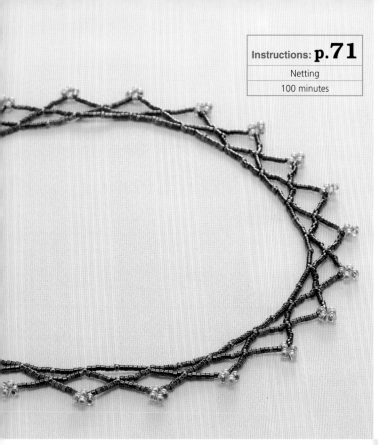

Instructions: **p.71**

Netting

100 minutes

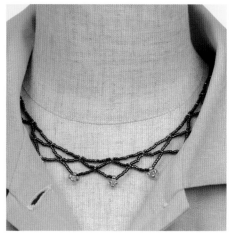

Christmas Tree Necklace

Design: Katayama Akiko

The inspiration for this simple necklace was a decorated Christmas tree against a night sky. It would be a fine choice for a beginner.

(For reference only)

Chevron stitch

Chain of Lace

Design: Kaifu Mihoko

This striking piece is made with the chevron stitch, a type of netting. Drop beads are elegant accents on this lacy necklace.

(For reference only)

Peyote stitch

Bouquet **N**ecklace

Design: Kisaki Yumi

This lovely necklace features flower
beads and cleverly designed fringe
(stems) with buds at their ends.

Instructions: **p.72**

Chevron stitch

60 minutes

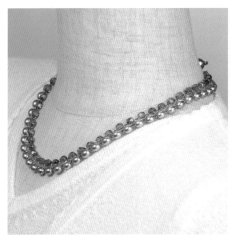

Elegant Necklace

Design: Gakushu Forum Design Research Group

This necklace is woven using the chevron stitch, a variation on netting, in a series of triangles. A very easy piece to make, we recommend it to beginners.

Chevron-Stitch Lariat

Design: Usami Junko

Like the elegant necklace shown above, this lariat is made with the chevron stitch. The ends are woven in mirror image with fire-polished and seed beads. This piece takes time to make, but its versatility makes it worth the effort.

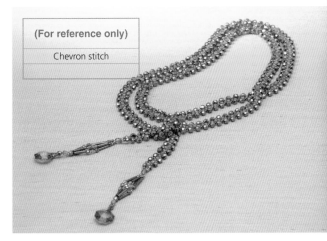

(For reference only)

Chevron stitch

Instructions: p.73

Herringbone stitch

150 minutes

Short Herringbone-Stitch Lariat

Design: Kudo Yumiko

We made a narrow cylinder, working in tubular herringbone stitch, incorporating magatama beads at regular intervals at the ends of this short lariat. This is another piece that takes time to make, but perhaps you, like us, will be mesmerized by the feel of the beads and the look of the piece as it evolves.

Spiral Necklace in Autumn Colors

(Also shown on p. 63)

■Finished length:

38cm (woven portion)

■Supplies

· 5.5m beading thread (see p. 74)
· 100 4-mm round glass pearl beads (lavender) #α387-6
· 300 2-mm seed beads (silver-lined translucent) #21(A)
· 300 2-mm seed beads (lavender AB) #166 (B)
· 321 2-mm seed beads (blue-violet) #1204 (C)
· 300 2-mm seed beads (pale blue-violet) #328 (D)
· 300 2-mm seed beads (violet-lined translucent) #928 (E)
· Trefoil hook-and-eye clasp (antique silver) #α4224SF

❶Cut a manageable length of thread. String a stopper bead on thread, leaving a 30-cm end. String 4 pearl beads (core beads) and 15 A seed beads (outer beads), referring to drawing. Pick up the 4 core beads (Fig. 1).

❷Add another core bead. Move outer beads strung in Step ① around to left. String 15 B seed beads and pick up 4 core beads from above (Fig. 2). Repeat, using C, D and E seed beads (outer beads) and then A, B, etc., in that order, to create subtle color shading, until you have 20 five-color patterns. When remaining thread is 20cm long, join new thread.

❸String 4 C seed beads (or another color, if your prefer), eye of clasp and 4 more C seed beads to form a loop. Pass needle back through loop beads again. Finish off thread, making half-hitch knots as you go (Fig. 3).

❹Remove stopper bead. String 6 seed beads, hook of clasp and 7 more seed beads, referring to drawing. Finish off thread (Fig. 4).

Long Spiral Necklace

(Also shown on p. 64)

■Finished length:

73cm (woven portion)

■Supplies

· 6m beading thread (see p. 74)
· 183 4-mm cube beads (matte black) #610
· 185 5-mm triangle beads (metallic black) #81
· 750 2-mm seed beads (silver) #713
· Feather-shaped hook-and-eye clasp (antique silver) #α4225S

❶Cut a manageable length of thread. String a stopper bead on thread, leaving a 30-cm end. String 3 triangle beads (core beads), then 2 seed beads, a cube bead and 2 more seed beads (outer beads), referring to drawing. Pick up the 3 core beads (Fig. 1).

❷String another core bead. Move outer beads strung in Step ① around to left. String another set of outer beads (2 seed beads, a cube bead and 2 more seed beads) and pick up 3 core beads from above (Fig. 2). Repeat until desired length is reached. When remaining thread is 20cm long, join new thread.

❸String 4 seed beads, eye of clasp and 5 more seed beads, referring to drawing. Finish off thread, running needle through beads, making half-hitch knots as you go (Fig. 3).

❹Remove stopper bead. String 4 seed beads, hook of clasp and 5 more seed beads. Pass needle through beads indicated in drawing again. Finish off thread (Fig. 4).

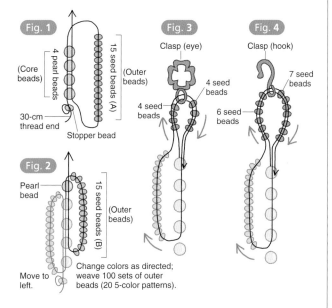

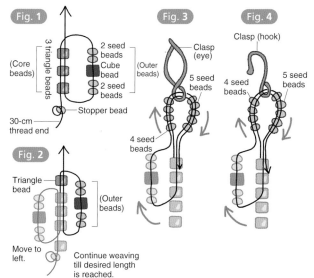

Christmas Tree Necklace

(Also shown on p. 66)

■Finished length:

43cm (netting: 41.5cm)

■Supplies

· 2.5m beading thread (see p. 74)
· 10-mm round lampwork bead (blue-green) #α 1976
· 908 Aiko beads (metallic blue-green) #TB506
· 84 3-mm seed beads (light gold) #989
· 97 2-mm seed beads (bronze) #221

❶String a stopper bead on thread, leaving a 30-cm end. Add 2 2-mm seed beads. String 6 Aiko beads, another 2-mm seed bead, 6 more Aiko beads and one more 2-mm seed bead (pattern beads). Repeat pattern twice. Add one 2-mm seed bead (Fig. 1).

❷Weave Row 1 of netting: string 7 Aiko beads, a 2-mm seed bead and 7 more Aiko beads on thread. Pick up every other 2-mm seed bead strung in Step ①. Repeat until you have reached beginning of work. Pick up first 2-mm seed bead strung (Fig. 2).

❸Make and attach clasp loop to beginning of work: string 3 2-mm seed beads, lampwork bead and another 2-mm seed bead. Pass needle through lampwork bead and 3 2-mm seed beads twice more. Pass needle through beads in Row 1 of netting, bringing it out where indicated in drawing (Fig. 3).

❹Weave Row 2 of netting. String 8 Aiko beads and 4 3-mm seed beads on thread. Pick up first 3-mm seed bead strung to form a picot, referring to drawing. Add 8 more Aiko beads and pick up a seed bead from Row 1 of netting. Repeat until you reach other end of necklace (Fig. 4).

❺Pick up last 7 Aiko beads in Row 1 of netting. Form a loop by stringing 23 2-mm seed beads. Pass needle through loop beads again, referring to drawing (Fig. 5). Finish off thread, passing needle back through netting and making half-hitch knots as you go. Remove stopper bead and finish off thread at beginning of work in the same way.

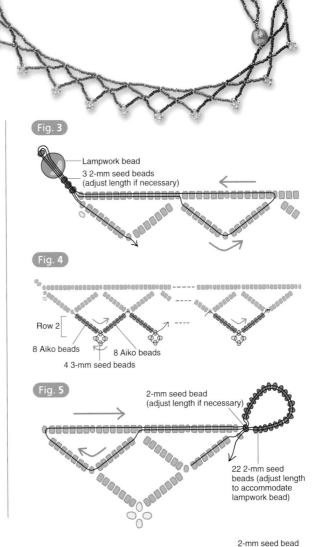

Fig. 3

Lampwork bead
3 2-mm seed beads
(adjust length if necessary)

Fig. 4

Row 2

8 Aiko beads
8 Aiko beads
4 3-mm seed beads

Fig. 5

2-mm seed bead
(adjust length if necessary)

22 2-mm seed beads (adjust length to accommodate lampwork bead)

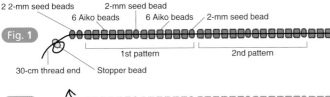

Fig. 1

2 2-mm seed beads
2-mm seed bead
6 Aiko beads
6 Aiko beads
2-mm seed bead
2-mm seed bead

1st pattern
2nd pattern
22nd pattern

30-cm thread end   Stopper bead

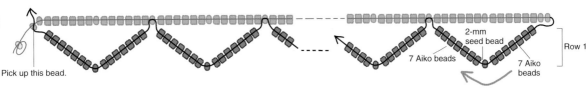

Fig. 2

Pick up this bead.

2-mm seed bead

7 Aiko beads   7 Aiko beads

Row 1

Elegant Necklace

(Also shown on p. 68)

■Finished length:

40cm (woven portion: 36.5cm)

■Supplies

· 2m beading thread (see p. 74)
· 50 5 x 6-mm oval glass pearl beads (pink) #α389-6
· 8-mm round glass pearl bead (pink) #α499-6
· 49 5-mm round fire-polished beads (mottled light amethyst) #α6605-35
· 100 3-mm bugle beads (silver-lined translucent) #21
· 139 2-mm seed beads (lavender) #746

❶String a stopper bead on thread, leaving a 30-cm end. String a seed bead, a bugle bead, another seed bead, an oval pearl bead, a seed bead and a bugle bead on thread. Pick up first seed bead strung, working in the opposite direction (Fig. 1).

❷String a fire-polished bead, a seed bead and a bugle bead on thread. Pick up seed bead above oval pearl bead, working outward, as shown in drawing (Fig. 2).

❸String an oval pearl bead, a seed bead and a bugle bead. Pick up seed bead above fire-polished bead, working outward (Fig. 3).

❹Repeat Steps ② and ③ until you've strung 50 oval pearl beads and 49 fire-polished beads. End with an oval pearl bead (Fig. 4).

❺Make half of clasp. String 6 seed beads, round pearl bead and 3 more seed beads on same thread. Pass needle back through pearl bead and 3 seed beads. Add 3 seed beads. Pick up beads indicated in drawing. Finish off thread, passing needle back through beads and making half-hitch knots as you go (Fig. 5).

❻Remove stopper bead. String 25 seed beads, forming a loop. Finish off thread as in Step ⑤ (Fig. 6).

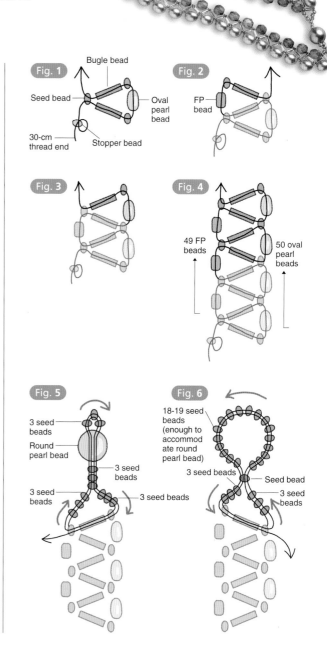

Fig. 1
Bugle bead
Seed bead
Oval pearl bead
30-cm thread end
Stopper bead

Fig. 2
FP bead

Fig. 3

Fig. 4
49 FP beads
50 oval pearl beads

Fig. 5
3 seed beads
Round pearl bead
3 seed beads
3 seed beads
3 seed beads

Fig. 6
18-19 seed beads (enough to accommodate round pearl bead)
3 seed beads
Seed bead
3 seed beads

Short Herringbone-Stitch Lariat

(Also shown on p. 69)

■Finished measurements:

72cm (woven portion: 65cm)

■Supplies

· 5.5m beading thread (see p. 74)
· 2,700 2-mm seed beads (blue) #997
· 40 4-mm magatama beads (silver-lined) #M21
· 40 4-mm magatama beads (aurora) #M161
· 40 4-mm magatama beads (blue) #M348
· 12 4-mm round glass pearl beads (blue) #α387-11
· 12 5 x 6-mm oval glass pearl beads (blue) #α389-11

*See p. 62 for supplies for Gold & Silver necklaces.

❶Cut a manageable length of thread. String a stopper bead, leaving an 80cm end. String 4 seed beads on thread. Pass needle through beads again in the same direction. Add 2 more seed beads and pick up 3rd and 4th seed beads strung. Repeat until you've made 6 2-bead ladder stitches (Fig. 1). See Steps ① - ③ on p. 54 for details about ladder stitch.

❷Pick up first and second seed beads. Close circle and pick up more beads as indicated in drawing (Fig. 2).

❸Now work in herringbone stitch. String 2 seed beads, then pick up seed beads in ladder stitch row, referring to drawings (Figs. 3 and 4). Repeat, then begin Row 2. Weave 4 rows, picking up seed beads from previous row as you go along (Figs. 5, 6).

❹Beginning with Row 5, incorporate the 3 colors of magatama beads into the piece, referring to drawing (Fig. 7).

❺After working 10 repetitions of the magatama bead pattern, weave 25cm without magatama beads. Then work another 10 repetitions of magatama bead pattern, and 4 rows without magatama beads. Finish with 2-bead ladder stitch as in Step ① (Fig. 8).

❻Use same thread to make fringe. String 10 seed beads, a round pearl bead, 6 seed beads, an oval pearl bead and 3 more seed beads. Pass needle back through beads, as shown in drawing. Make 5 more strands of fringe. Finish off thread, passing needle back through beads in lariat (Fig. 9).

❼Remove stopper bead. Make fringe as in Step ⑥. Finish off thread.

> **T I P**
>
> When you have only 20cm thread left, join new thread. Pick up beads, starting in the 10th row from the end, making half-hitch knots as you go. When you reach end of piece, cut thread at the edge of a bead.

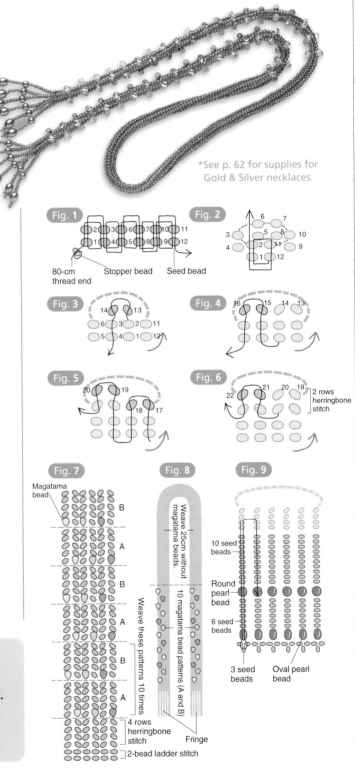

Fig. 1
80-cm thread end   Stopper bead   Seed bead

Fig. 2

Fig. 3

Fig. 4

Fig. 5

Fig. 6
2 rows herringbone stitch

Fig. 7
Magatama bead
B
A
B
A
B
A
Weave these patterns 10 times
4 rows herringbone stitch
2-bead ladder stitch

Fig. 8
Weave 25cm without magatama beads.
10 magatama bead patterns (A and B)
Fringe

Fig. 9
10 seed beads
Round pearl bead
6 seed beads
3 seed beads   Oval pearl bead

TOOLS AND SUPPLIES FOR OFFLOOM BEADWEAVING

You don't need cumbersome or expensive equipment or supplies for off-loom beadweaving. That's part of what makes this type of beadwork so attractive. To start out, all you need are needles, thread and beads.

Beading needles

The needles commonly used for off-loom beadweaving are beading needles in sizes 10, 11 and 12. The larger the number, the finer the needle. These needles come in various lengths, from 3cm to 5cm. Longer needles are convenient when you need to string a lot of beads at once. The shorter needles come in handy when you're finishing off thread or picking up one bead in the middle of a woven piece. Toho, Clover, John James and Sharps are some of the leading brands.

Beading thread

The needles commonly used for off-loom beadweaving are beading needles in sizes 10, 11 and 12. The larger the number, the finer the needle. These needles come in various lengths, from 3cm to 5cm. Longer needles are convenient when you need to string a lot of beads at once. The shorter needles come in handy when you're finishing off thread or picking up one bead in the middle of a woven piece. Toho, Clover, John James and Sharps are some of the leading brands.

Other tools

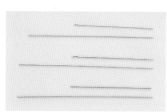

Scissors
You'll need embroidery scissors for cutting lengths of thread, and thread nippers for clipping thread ends.

Beading mats
These offer a cushioned work surface, and keep beads from rolling around.

Tape measure
You'll definitely need one of these for measuring thread and woven pieces.

Flat-nose pliers
Used to open and close jump rings and other findings.

Beads

Seed beads
These small cylindrical beads range in size from 1.5mm to 4mm.

Polygonal beads
This class of beads includes triangle, cube and hex (hexagonal) beads. All of them have round holes.

Bugle beads
The most common sizes of these long cylindrical beads are 3mm and 6mm.

3-cut beads
Irregular cuts on their surfaces cause these beads to sparkle beautifully in the light.

Magatama beads
These are drop beads with off-center holes.

Fire-polished beads
Polished over an open fire, these beads have rounded facets and a special luster.

Pearl beads
Both real pearl beads (including freshwater pearl beads) and glass imitations are available.

Crystal beads
The most famous manufacturer of these faceted beads is the Austrian firm Swarovski.

Basic **off-loom beadweaving** techniques

In this section we introduce basic techniques that should be learned before you make jewelry. They are not difficult, and mastering them will make your work easier. It's a good idea to practice them, so you get used to handling the needle and thread.

Cutting the thread

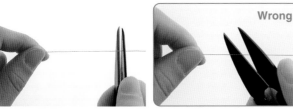

Wrong

If you're using nylon thread, hold the scissors so they (re perpendicular to the thread (don't cut on an angle).

Preparing the thread

To remove kinks from nylon thread, hold a 40-cm length in both hands and pull hard. Do this before you use the thread.

Stringing beads

Place a bead on a beading mat. With the point of the needle, turn the bead on its side. Insert needle into hole in bead.

■Moving beads

To move beads that you've already strung, hold on to the beads and pull on the thread. Always move the thread, not the beads.

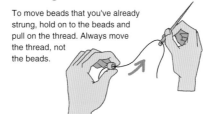

Wrong

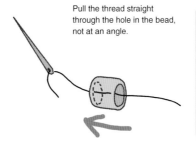

Passing through beads

Here we refer to passing the needle through beads that have already been strung or woven. Place woven piece between your fingers, as shown in photo. Pass needle through bead (or beads), taking care not to sew through the thread. If the beads seem loose, pull on the thread extending from them.

Pulling the thread

Pull the thread straight through the hole in the bead, not at an angle.

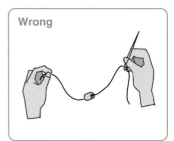

Wrong

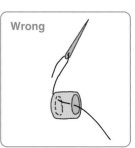

Stopper bead

Attach a stopper bead to the thread before you begin work. It keeps the beads you string afterwards from falling off. You'll be removing it later, so the color doesn't matter. Seed beads (the 2-mm size) seem to work best.

■Attaching a stopper bead

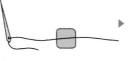

①String stopper bead on thread.

②Pass needle through stopper bead again from same direction.

③Leaving the specified length of thread at the end, pull thread to secure stopper bead.

THE BASIC STITCHES

Here we introduce nine basic stitches used in off-loom beadweaving. Besides showing you how to make the stitches, we show you how to count stitches and rows, make increases and decreases, and finish off thread. In this book we have not covered every off-loom stitch and technique, but you will find other stitches and techniques much more accessible once you have mastered the ones we introduce.

You will also be ready to make your own designs and, of course, create your own beautiful jewelry.

Peyote stitch

Flat peyote stitch (even-count)

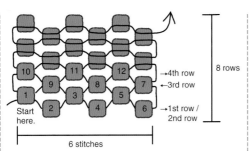

Beads for Rows 1 and 2 are strung at the same time. In Row 3, you string a new bead, skip a bead on the previous row, and pick up the next one. Starting with Row 4, you pick up the beads that protrude from the preceding row.

Flat peyote stitch (odd-count)

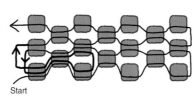

When you have no next bead to go to, you will need to make turns in some of the beads already strung so that you can start the next row.

Finishing off thread

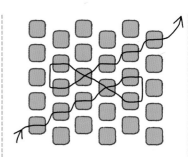

Pass needle back through beads on the diagonal, forming intersections two or three times. Cut thread.

Making a one-stitch increase at an edge

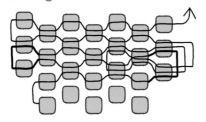

String 2 beads at the edge.

Making a one-stitch decrease at an edge

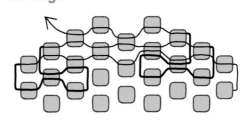

Make turns as you would with odd-count peyote stitch. The thread should go into the bead at the edge on the diagonal.

Tubular peyote stitch (even-count) step up

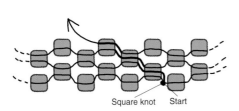

To prepare for the next row, pass needle through first bead picked up in row and first bead strung.

Tubular peyote stitch (odd-count) spiral

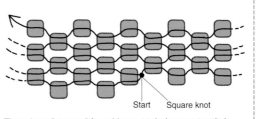

There is no "step up" for odd-count tubular peyote stitch.

■Making an increase

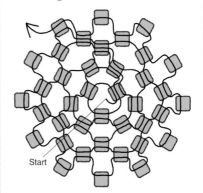

String 2 beads where you wish to make the increase. On the next row, pick up these 2 beads separately.

■Making a decrease

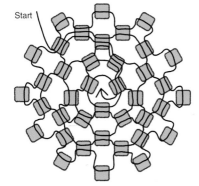

Pick up 2 beads at the same time where you wish to make the decrease. On the next row, string only one bead.

■Joining edges

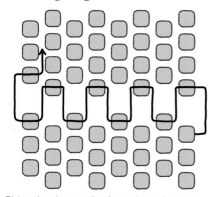

Pick up beads protruding from edges, alternating between the two. Pull thread after picking up each bead.

Ladder stitch

■One-bead ladder stitch

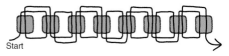

Ladder stitch is often used at the beginning of brick and herringbone-stitch weaving.

■Two-bead ladder stitch

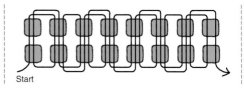

Brick stitch

■Flat peyote stitch (even-count)

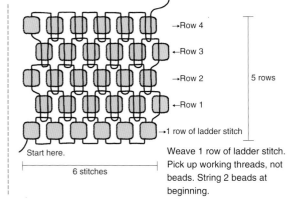

→Row 4
←Row 3
→Row 2
←Row 1
→1 row of ladder stitch
5 rows
6 stitches

Weave 1 row of ladder stitch. Pick up working threads, not beads. String 2 beads at beginning.

■Finishing off thread

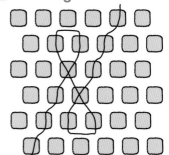

Pass needle back through beads on the diagonal, forming intersections two or three times. Cut thread.

■Making a one-stitch increase at each edge

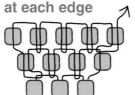

On the edge where you began work, string 2 beads and pick up working thread between last 2 beads on previous row. On opposite edge, pick up last working thread twice.

■Making a one-stitch decrease at each edge

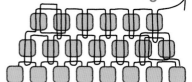

On the edge where you began work, string 2 beads, then pick up second working thread. Work as in ladder stitch (down and back up through beads) to straighten and stabilize beads. On opposite edge, pick up working thread only once.

Herringbone stitch

Flat herringbone stitch

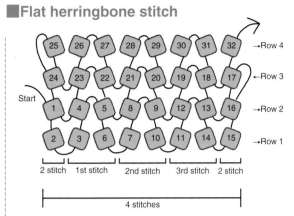

String beads for Rows 1 and 2 all at once. Work in pattern starting with Row 3. You will have a half stitch at each edge.

Flat herringbone stitch (ladder-stitch beginning)

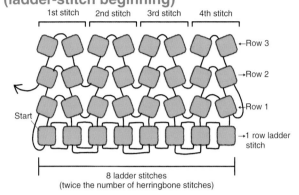

Weave one row of ladder stitch. You will have whole stitches at the edges.

Finishing off thread

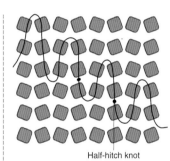

Half-hitch knot

Run needle vertically through beads. Make half-hitch knots between beads.

Making a half-stitch increase at an edge

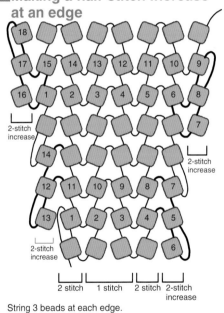

String 3 beads at each edge.

Making a half-stitch decrease at an edge

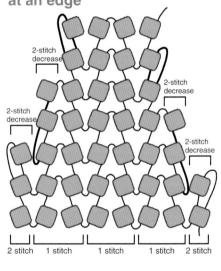

Don't pick up half stitches at edges.

Tubular herringbone stitch step up (herringbone stitch beginning)

Square knot

String beads for first row. Join first and last beads to close circle. Work in herringbone stitch starting with Row 2.

Tubular herringbone stitch step up (ladder-stitch beginning)

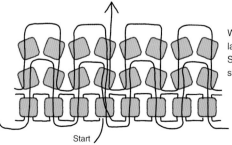

Start

Work first row in ladder stitch. Switch to herringbone stitch in Row 2.

■Tubular spiral herringbone stitch

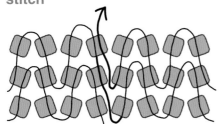

Weave in a spiral pattern. There is no step up for this stitch.

■Circular herringbone stitch

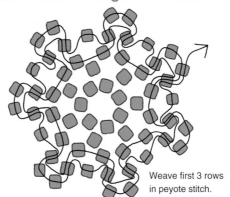

Weave first 3 rows in peyote stitch.

Netting

■Flat netting (vertical)

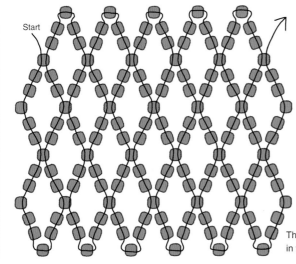

Start

Thread is perpendicular to the direction in which the work progresses.

■Flat netting (horizontal)

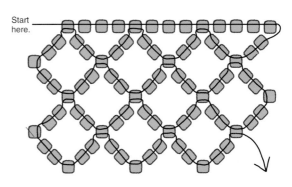

Start here.

Thread is parallel to the direction in which the work progresses.

Basic stitches

Right-angle weave stitch

■Flat right-angle weave (even-count)

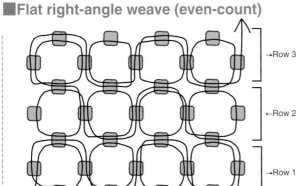

→Row 3

←Row 2

→Row 1

Start

1st stitch   2nd stitch   3rd stitch   4th stitch

String 4 beads to form a circle, then pick up 2 of them again. Starting with the 2nd stitch, string 3 beads at a time. In Row 2, connect new stitches to stitches in preceding row.

■Flat right-angle weave stitch (odd-count)

After working the last stitch, pick up only the last bead added, then begin next row.

Square stitch

■Flat square stitch

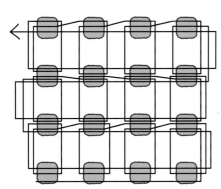

After completing a row, pass needle through beads in previous row and row just completed.

Spiral rope stitch

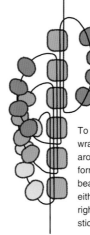

Start

To work this stitch, you wrap outer beads around core beads to form a spiral. Outer beads can be wrapped either to the left or right, as long as you stick to one direction.

■Finishing off thread

If the core beads have small holes, run your needle through the outer beads to finish off the thread.

Half-hitch knot

Daisy chain stitch

■Open daisy chain stitch

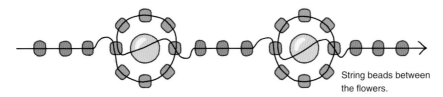

String beads between the flowers.

■Continuous daisy chain stitch connected by one bead

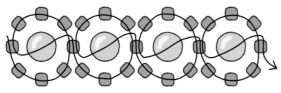

One "petal" is shared by adjacent daisies.

■Continuous daisy chain stitch connected by 2 beads

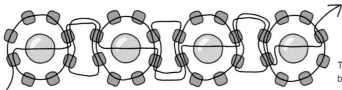

Two "petals" are shared by adjacent daisies.